The Crown of Individuality

By

William George Jordan

Published by Forgotten Books 2012

PIBN 1000126367

THE CROWN OF INDIVIDUALITY

THE CROWN OF INDIVIDUALITY

by

WILLIAM
GEORGE
JORDAN

FLEMING H.
REVELL
COMPANY

CHICAGO
TORONTO

NEW YORK

LONDON
EDINBURGH

CONTENTS

The Crown of Individuality

HE supreme courage of life is the courage of the soul. It is living, day by day, sincerely, steadfastly, serenely,—despite all opinions, all obstacles, all opposition. It means the wine of inspiration for ourselves and others that comes from the crushed grapes of our sorrows. This courage makes the simplest life, great; it makes the greatest life—sublime. It means the royal dignity of fine individual living.

Every man reigns a king over the kingdom of—self. He wears the crown of individuality that no hands but his own can ever remove. He should not only reign, but—rule. His individuality is his true self, his best self, his highest self, his self victorious. His thoughts, his words, his acts, his feelings, his aims and his powers are his —subjects. With gentle, firm strength he must command them or, they will finally take from his feeble fingers the reins of government and rule in his stead. Man must first be true to himself or he will be false to all the world.

Man reigns over this miniature kingdom of self—alone. He is as much an autocrat as is God in ruling the universe. No one can make him good or evil but he, himself. No one else in all the world has his work or his influence. Each of us can carry a balm of joy, and strength, and light, and love to some hearts that will respond to no other. Each can add the last bitter drop in the cup of life to some one dependent on us through love or friendship. No other in all the world can live our life, loyally fulfill our duties, or wear the crown of our individuality. It is a wondrous joy and inspiration to us if we see this in its true light, for never again would we ask: "What use am I in the world?"

When God "created man in His own image" His first gift to him was—dominion. The greatest dominion is over —self. Our lives should be vital to those around us. Each of us can be the sun of life in the sky of some one —perhaps many. Were we suddenly to have made luminant to us in every vivid detail our daily influence we should stand stunned by the revelation as was Moses in reverent expectancy before the burning bush.

The realization of the glory of the crown of our individuality would sweep the pettiness of selfish living and the wonder of the unanswerable eternal problems alike into—nothingness.

The world needs more individuality in its men and women. It needs them with the joy of individual freedom in their minds, the fresh blood of honest purpose in their hearts, and the courage of truth in their souls. It needs more people daring to think their own highest thoughts and strong vibrant voices to speak them, not human phonographs mechanically giving forth what some one else has talked into them. The world needs men and women led by the light of truth alone, and as powerless to suppress their highest convictions as Vesuvius to restrain its living fire.

They have the glad inspiring consciousness that they are not mere units on the census list, not weak victims of their own impulses, not human bricks baked into deadly uniformity by conventionality, but themselves—individuals. They are not faint carbon copies of others but strong, bold-print originals,—of themselves. They are ever lights not reflections, voices not echoes. To them the real things of life are the only great ones, the only objects worth a hard struggle.

In our darkest hours new strength always comes to us, if we believe, as the silent stars shine out in the sky above us—when it is dark enough. The hardest battle for our highest self

is, when hungry for love and companionship of the soul, we must fight on
—alone. If we have one or two dear loyal ones watching bravely by our side, understanding us with a look, heartening us with a smile or inspiring us with a warm hand-pressure, we should fairly tingle with courage and confidence.

But if these leave us, slip away under the strain, or even betray us, let us face alone the seemingly empty life that is left us, just as heroically as we can. Let us still stand in silent strength, like a lone sentry keeping guard over a sleeping regiment, in the grim shadows of night, forgetting for a time the terror of the solitude, the darkness, the loneliness, the isolation and the phantom invasion of memories that will not stay buried, in the courage that comes from facing an inevitable duty with a sturdy soul. Of course it is not easy to live on the uplands of life. It was never intended to be easy, but oh—it is worth while.

Individuality is the only real life. It is breathing the ozone of mental, moral, spiritual freedom. Nature made the countless thousands of flowers, trees, birds and animals without permitting two to be precisely alike. She stamped them with—individuality. She did it in a greater way for man. Some people seem to spend most of their time—trying to soak off the stamp. They follow in the footsteps of the crowd, guided by their advice. They wear a uniform of opinion ; suffer in the strait-jacket of silly convention, seek ever to keep in step with the line, and march in solid sameness along the comfortably paved road of other people's thinking, —not their own.

Individuality means stimulating all the flowers of our best nature and banishing one by one the weeds of our lower self. It means kingship over self and kinship with all humanity. It means self-knowledge, self-confidence, self-reliance, self-poise, self-control, self-conquest. It is the fullest expression of our highest self, as the most perfect rose most truly represents the bush from which it blossoms.

Individuality is the complete self-acting union and unity of man's whole mind, nature, heart and life. It is moved ever from within, not from without. The automobile is a type of individuality—it is neither pushed, pulled nor propelled by outside forces.

The automobile is self-inspired, self-directed, self-moving.

Eccentricity is not individuality—it is a warped, unnatural distortion, like a reflection from a concave or convex mirror. Hypocrisy is not individuality—a mask is never a face and no matter how close it be held to the skin it never becomes a real face. Conventionality is not individuality—it is the molding of all that is vital and original in us to conform to an average type. Affectation is not individuality—it is only pretentious display of qualities one has not in stock. Individuality permeates every thought, word and act of ours as a half grain of aniline will tinge a hogshead of water so that the microscope will detect the colouring matter in every drop. Individuality crowns every expression of itself, in every day of living, with the —crown of its own kingship.

He who is swerved from a course he knows is right, through fear of ridicule, taunts, sneers or sarcasm of those around him, is not a man—self-directed by right. He is only a weak puppet pulled by the strings of manipulation in the hands of others. He is a figure in a moral Punch and Judy show— without its entertaining quality.

The man who knows he is doing wrong, may realize it coolly, calmly, considerately, and even confess it with a sort of bravado, while he is too cowardly and selfish to do the imperative right is not—a king over his higher self but a weak slave of his lower self. That he knows the right and sees it without illusion merely emphasizes the depth of the abyss into which he has fallen.

The woman who lets bitterness grow in her heart until it poisons judgment, kills the love that was dear to her, deadens all her finer emotions and lets petrified prejudice usurp the throne of her justice while she shuts her ears to all pleas for understanding, commits one of those little tragedies in every-day life that may scar for years the soul of the one so cruelly misjudged. She may recklessly throw the golden crown of her individuality, with all its dear, sweet love and tenderness, into the weary loneliness of the years.

He who, from sheer lack of purpose, drifts through life, letting the golden years of his highest hopes glide empty back into the perspective of his past while he fills his ears with the lorelei song of procrastination is working overtime in accumulating remorse to darken his future. He is idly permitting the crown of his individuality to remain an irritating symbol of what *might be* rather than a joyous emblem of what *is*. This man is reigning, for reign he must, but he is not— ruling.

Individuality does not mean merely being our self, but our—highest self. It never means living for self alone. The world, in every phase, must be saved by—individuals. You cannot take humanity in mass up in moral elevators; they must receive and accept good as individuals. The united work of individuals makes up the action of society. It is easier to stimulate the individual to action than it is to galvanize society, as it is easier to lift one stone than a cathedral. As we intensify true individuality we at the same instant begin a fine cooperation with the best work of all humanity.

Individuality is the link; cooperation is the chain. You can strengthen the chain only as you strengthen the link. Christ, the great individualist, knew no shadow of selfishness. He sought to make better, stronger links in the living chain of humanity. His influence was ever an inspiration. He represented perfected individuality and individual perfection.

Let us reign a king over our individuality by conquering every element of weakness within us that keeps us from our best and raising every element of strength to its highest power by living in simple harmony with our ideals. We should begin it to-day. To-day is the only real day of life for us. To-day is the tomb of yesterday, the cradle of to-morrow. All our past ends in to-day. All our future begins in to-day.

Let us seek to reign nobly on the throne of our highest self for just a single day, filling every moment of every hour with our finest, unselfish best. Then there would come to us such a vision of the golden glory of the sunlit heights, such a glad, glowing tonic of the higher levels of life, that we could never dwell again in the darkened valley of ordinary living without feeling shut in, stifled, and hungry for the freer air and the broader outlook.

If at the close of day we can think of even *one* human being whose sky has been darkened by our selfishness, one whose burden has been new-weighted by our unkindness, one whose pillow will be wet with sobs for our injustice, one whose faith in humanity has been weakened at a crucial moment by our bitterness or cruelty, let us make quick atonement. Let us write the letter our heart impels us to write, while foolish pride would stay the hand; let us speak the confession that will glorify the lips we fear it may humiliate; let us stretch out the hand of love in the darkness till it touches and inspires the faithful one that possibly never caused us real pain.

Let us have that great pride in our individuality that would scorn to let petty pique or vanity keep us from doing what we know is right. Wear the robes of your royal pride in such kingly fashion that it would seem no sacrifice to stoop to brush off that which might stain them.

Let us make this life of ours a joy to ourselves and a tower of strength to others. Then shall we have made this life a success, no matter what its results. We shall have made character—and character is real life. The truest success is not the one the world often holds highest—that which is rung up on a cash-register. The truest success is a strong nature, living at a high but steady moral pressure, and radiating love, kindness, sympathy, strength, tenderness and joy to others.

Let us live with our faces turned ever courageously to the East for the faintest sunrise of new inspiration. Let us realize that the four guardians of the crown of individuality are Right, Justice, Truth, and Love. Let us make Right our highest guide, Justice our finest aim, Truth our final revelation, and Love the constant atmosphere of our living. Then truly will we reign and—rule. It is not the extent of the kingdom but the fine quality of the kingship that really counts.

II

No Room for Them in the Inn

HE world's attitude towards the birth of every great truth is focused in a single phrase in the simple story of the first Christmas, the greatest birthday since Time began. Mary laid the infant Christ in a manger—"because there was no room for them in the inn."

For worldly success, fame, social prestige, laurel-crowned triumph, the inn is illuminated; welcoming music fills the air; and the inn doors are thrown wide open. But struggle towards sublime attainment, heroic ef-

fort to better the world, simple conse-
cration of soul to a noble ideal means
—the manger and a lonely pathway lit
only by the torch of truth held high
in the hand of purpose.

Right must ever fight its way
against the world. Truth must ever
walk alone in its Gethsemane. Justice
must bravely face its Calvary if it
would still live in triumph after all
efforts to slay it. Love must ever, in
the end, burst forth in its splendour
from the dark clouds of hate and dis-
cord that seek to obscure it. These
great truths must be born in the
manger of poverty, or pain, or trial, or
suffering, finding no room at the inn
until at last by entering it in triumph
they honour the inn that never
honoured them in their hours of need,
of struggle or of darkness.

It is so written in the story of the world's leaders, it is the chorus of the song of every great human effort, it is the secret of the loneliest hours of supreme aspiration, it epitomizes the whole life of Christ. As a babe— there was no room for Him in the inn; as a boy—there was no room for Him in Israel; as a man, condemned by Pilate—there was no room for Him in all the world. His life seemed a failure, the results poor and barren, yet to-day the world has thousands of churches, spiritual inns, built in His memory. The glory of the end makes trials along the way seem—nothing.

It requires sterling courage to live on the uplands of truth, battling bravely for the right, undismayed by coldness, undaunted by contempt, unmoved by criticism, serenely confident,

even in the darkest hours, that right,
justice and truth must win in the end.

We may see the inn welcome the
successful without auditing the ac-
counts of ways and means by which
that success was won ; pass in the
hypocrite without realizing that his
passport is forged, accept the swagger-
ing and assertive at their own estimate,
near-sightedly mistake the brass of
pretense for the gold of true worth,
give a fine suite of corner rooms to a
fad and have no room at all for a
philosophy. The world makes many
mistakes. Time corrects many mis-
takes. Time is always on the side of
right and truth. It is the silent ally
of all great work.

There comes a time in every indi-
vidual life when earnest, honest effort,
disheartened,   dismayed,   distressed,

says: "What is the use of it all?
Why should I suffer poverty, sorrow,
loneliness and failure while I am try-
ing so hard to be good, kind, sympa-
thetic, helpful, and just? Why should
I not have some of the good things I
long for? Is the struggle for moral
things really worth while after all?"

These are big questions; they are
the very sobs of the soul. They are
hard indeed to answer, but something
within us, deeper than reason, tells us
that it is worth while, that it must be
and that we must set our feet bravely
towards the future and do our best even
when the clouds hang lowest. The
seeming ease and prosperity of those
leading idle, selfish lives should never
divert us from the path of truth.

If we know we are right we should
care naught for the crowd at the inn.

It must be that there is something
higher in life than the welcome at the
inn, the approval of the world, or
any accumulation of purely material
things. There is the consciousness of
work well done, of steadfast loyalty to
an ideal, of faithfulness in little things,
of lives made sweeter, truer, better by
our living, of a lovelight in eyes look-
ing into ours—these may be part of the
glorious flowering of our days greater
far to our highest self than any mere
welcome at the inn.

Moral goodness or spiritual glow does
not bring—worldly success. That it
does is a delusive yet popular system of
ethics. Daily exercise of all the higher
virtues and keeping one's moral muscles
in prime condition does not necessarily
bring—wealth and prosperity. If it
were true the saints of the world would

be the millionaires. Careful study of
our richest class does not show they are
conspicuous wearers of halos. If it
were true, it would be placing the ma-
terial side of life as the ideal, the goal,
the aim, and end of living. High
moral or spiritual life would be but a
means, morality would be but a shrewd
investment, prosperity a dividend.

He who speculates in morals for the
coupons and trading stamps of success
is not really moral, he is merely—
hypocritic. Business success is the re-
sult of obeying, in some form, specific
laws that make that success. Some of
these laws are based on those of morals,
some run parallel, some cut across
morals on the bias, but they are not—
identical. The angel Gabriel would
probably not be able to make day's
wages in Wall Street. Christ had not

"where to lay His head." The only
reason for being right, doing right, and
living right is—because it is right.

True living brings peace to the soul,
fibre to character, kingship over self, in-
spiration to others, but not necessarily—
money and material prosperity. These
are surely pleasing to possess; few
people are trying very energetically to
dodge them. They have their proper
place in the scheme of life but they are
not—supreme. If they were highest,
candidates for the choicest seats in
heaven could be selected purely by
double "A" Bradstreet ratings; they
would be taken ever from the crowded
inn—not the lonely manger. At the
inn they inquire: "Will it pay? Is it
popular? Is it successful?" At the
manger they ask: "Is it right? Is it
true? Is it helpful?"

True living consists of living at our best without thought of reward—doing the highest right, as we see it, and facing results, calmly, courageously and unquestioning. It means living to give not to get, thinking more of what we can radiate than what we can absorb, more of what we are than of what we have.

Humanity dreams golden dreams of the wondrous things it would do if it only had money—the happiness, cheer, comfort, joy and peace it could bring to thousands. But wealth could not buy the very things the world hungers for most—love, kindness, calmness, inspiration, peace, trust, truth and justice. The greatest gift the individual can give the world is—personal service. The manger typified personal service, consecrated freely to humanity.

Every great truth in all the ages
has had to battle for recognition. If
it be real it is worth the struggle.
Out of the struggle comes new strength
for the victor. Trampled grass grows
the greenest. Hardship and trial and
restriction and opposition mean new
vitality to character. In potting plants
it is well not to have the pot too large,
for the more crowded the roots the
more the plant will bloom. It is true,
in a larger sense, of life. The world
has ever misunderstood and battled
against its thinkers, its leaders, its
reformers, its heroes.

We must all fight for our ideals, for
truth, for individuality, never counting
the cost, never keeping our ears close to
the ground to hear the faint murmurs
of approval or condemnation from the
self-absorbed crowd at the inn.

If confident that we are right, according to our highest light, if we are sailing by our chart, guided by our compass, freighted with a true cargo and headed for our harbour let us care naught for what the world says. What matters it if the world thinks our economy for some unselfish purpose known to us alone is meanness, our loyalty to an ideal is folly, our decision of a right is the climax of error and the joy that is nearest and dearest but an empty dream?

The world ever comes round at last to the point of view of the man who is right. The inn finally finds room for truth and right—when they have proved themselves. The manger and the lonely path are ever—finally vindicated. It is the final surrender to—the crown of individuality.

III

Facing the Mistakes *of* Life

HERE are only two classes of people who never make mistakes, —they are the dead and the unborn. Mistakes are the inevitable accompaniment of the greatest gift given to man,—individual freedom of action. If he were only a pawn in the fingers of Omnipotence, with no self-moving power, man would never make a mistake, but his very immunity would degrade him to the ranks of the lower animals and the plants. An oyster never makes a mistake,—it has not the mind that would permit it to forsake an instinct.

Let us be glad of the dignity of our privilege to make mistakes, glad of the wisdom that enables us to recognize them, glad of the power that permits us to turn their light as a glowing illumination along the pathway of our future.

Mistakes are the growing pains of wisdom, the assessments we pay on our stock of experience, the raw material of error to be transformed into higher living.   Without them there would be no individual growth, no progress, no conquest.   Mistakes are the knots, the tangles, the broken threads, the dropped stitches in the web of our living.   They are the misdeals in judgment, our unwise investments in morals, the profit and loss account of wisdom.   They are the misleading by-paths from the straight road of truth—

and truth in our highest living is but the accuracy of the soul.

Human fallibility, weakness, pettiness, folly and sin are all—mistakes. They are to be accepted as mortgages of error, to be redeemed by wiser living. They should never weakly be taken as justifying bankruptcy of effort. Even a great mistake is only an episode —never a whole life.

Life is simply time given to man to learn how to live. Mistakes are always part of learning. The real dignity of life consists in cultivating a fine attitude towards our own mistakes and those of others. It is the fine tolerance of a fine soul. Man becomes great, not through never making mistakes, but by profiting by those he does make; by being satisfied with a single rendition of a mistake, not en-

coring it into a continuous perform-
ance; by getting from it the honey of
new, regenerating inspiration with no
irritating sting of morbid regret; by
building better to-day because of his
poor yesterday; and by rising with re-
newed strength, finer purpose and
freshened courage every time he falls.

In great chain factories, power ma-
chines are specially built to test chains
—to make them fail, to show their
weakness, to reveal the mistakes of
workmanship. Let us thank God
when a mistake shows us the weak
link in the chain of our living. It is
a new revelation of how to live. It
means the rich red blood of a new in-
spiration.

If we have made an error, done a
wrong, been unjust to another or to
ourselves, or, like the Pharisee, passed

by some opportunity for good, we should have the courage to face our mistake squarely, to call it boldly by its right name, to acknowledge it frankly and to put in no flimsy alibis of excuse to˘protect an anæmic self-esteem.

If we have been selfish, unselfishness should atone ; if we have wronged, we should right ; if we have hurt, we should heal ; if we have taken unjustly, we should restore ; if we have been unfair, we should become just.   Regret without regeneration is—an emotional gold-brick.   Every possible reparation should be made.   If confession of regret for the wrong and for our inability to set it right be the maximum of our power let us at least do that.   A quick atonement sometimes almost effaces the memory.   If foolish pride stands in our way we are aggravating the first mistake by a new one. Some people's mistakes are never born singly—they come in litters.

Those who waken to the realization of their wrong act, weeks, months or years later, sometimes feel it is better to let confession or reparation lapse, that it is too late to reopen a closed account; but men rarely feel deeply wounded if asked to accept payment on an old promissory note—outlawed for years.

Some people like to wander in the cemetery of their past errors, to reread the old epitaphs and to spend hours in mourning over the grave of a wrong. This new mistake does not antidote the old one. The remorse that paralyzes hope, corrodes purpose, and deadens energy is not moral health, it is— an indigestion of the soul that cannot

assimilate an act. It is selfish, cow-
ardly surrender to the dominance of
the past. It is lost motion in morals ;
it does no good to the individual, to
the injured, to others, or to the world.
If the past be unworthy live it down ;
if it be worthy live up to it and—
surpass it.

Omnipotence cannot change the past,
so why should *we* try ? Our duty is to
compel that past to vitalize our future
with new courage and purpose, making
it a larger, greater future than would
have been possible without the past
that has so grieved us. If we can get
real, fine, appetizing dividends from
our mistakes they prove themselves not
losses but—wise investments. They
seem like old mining shares, laid aside
in the lavender of memory of our
optimism and now, by some sudden

change in the market of speculation, proved to be of real value.

Realizing mistakes is good; realizing on them is better. When a captain finds his vessel is out of the right channel, carried, by negligence, by adverse winds or by blundering through a fog, from the true course, he wastes no time in bemoaning his mistake but at the first sunburst takes new bearings, changes his course, steers bravely towards his harbour with renewed courage to make up the time he has lost. The mistake means—increased care and greater speed.

Musing over the dreams of youth, the golden hopes that have not blossomed into deeds, is a dangerous mental dissipation. In very small doses it may stimulate; in large ones it weakens effort. It over-emphasizes the past

at the expense of the present; it adds
weights, not wings, to purpose. "It
might have been" is the lullaby of
regret with which man often puts to
sleep the mighty courage and confi-
dence that should inspire him. We
do not need narcotics in life so much
as we need tonics. We may try some-
times, sadly and speculatively, to re-
construct our life from some date in
the past when we might have taken a
different course. We build on a dead
"if." This is the most unwise brand
of air-castle.

We go back in memory to some fork
of the road in life and think what
would have happened and how won-
drously better it would have been had
we taken the other turning of the
road. "If we had learned some other
business;" "If we had gone West in

1884 ; " " If we had married the other one ; " " If we had bought telephone stock when it was at 35 ; " " If we had taken a different course in education ; " " If we had only spent certain money in some other way,"—and so we run uselessly our empty train of thought over these slippery " ifs."

Even if these courses might have been wiser, and we do not really know, it is now as impossible to change back to them as for the human race to go back to the original bit of protoplasm from which science declares we are evolved. The past does not belong to us to change or to modify; it is only the golden present that is ours to make as we would wish. The present is raw material; the past is finished product, —finished forever for good or ill. No regret will ever enable us to relive it.

The other road always looks attract-
ive. Distant sails are always white;
far-off hills always green. It may per-
haps have been the poorer road after
all, could our imagination, through
some magic, see with perfect vision the
finality of its possibility. The other
road might have meant wealth but less
happiness; fame might have charmed
our ears with the sweet music of praise,
but the little hand of love that rests so
trustingly in ours might have been
denied us. Death itself might have
come earlier to us or his touch stilled
the beatings of a heart we hold dearer
than our own. What the other road
might have meant no eternity of con-
jecture could ever reveal; no omnipo-
tence could enable us now to walk
therein even if we wished.

We cannot relive our old mistakes,

but we can make them the means of future immunity from the folly that caused them. If we were impatient yesterday, it should inspire us to be patient to-day. Yesterday's anger may be the seed of to-day's sweetness. To-day's kindness should be the form assumed by our regret at yesterday's cruelty. Our unfairness to one may open our eyes to the possibility of greater fairness to hundreds. Injustice to one that may seem to have cost us much may really have cost us little if it make us more kind, tender and thoughtful for long years.

It is a greater mistake to err in purpose, in aim, in principle, than in our method of attaining them. The method may readily be modified ; to change the purpose may upset the whole plan of our life. It is easier in mid-ocean to vary the course of the ship than to change the cargo.

Right principles are vital and primary. They bring the maximum of profit from mistakes, reduce the loss to a minimum. False pride perpetuates our mistakes, deters us from confessing them, debars us from repairing them and ceasing them.

Man's attitude towards his mistakes is various and peculiar; some do not see them; some will not see them; some see without changing; some see and deplore, but keep on; some make the same mistakes over and over again, in principle not in form; some blame others for their own mistakes; some condemn others for mistakes seemingly unconscious that they themselves are committing similar ones; some excuse their mistakes by saying that others do the same things, as though a disease were less dangerous when it becomes —epidemic in a community.

Failure does not necessarily imply a mistake. If we have held our standard high, bravely fought a good fight for the right, held our part courageously against heavy opposition and have finally seen the citadel of our great hope taken by superior force, by overwhelming conditions, or sapped and undermined by jealousy, envy or treachery we have met with failure, it is true, but—we have not made a mistake.

The world may condemn us for this non-success. What does the silly, babbling, unthinking world, that has not seen our heroic efforts, know about it? What does it matter what the world thinks, or says, if we know we have done our best? Sometimes men fail nobly because they have the courage to forego triumph at the cost of character, honour, truth and justice.

Let us never accept mistakes as final ; let us organize victory out of the broken ranks of failure and, despite all odds, fight on calmly, courageously, unflinchingly, serenely confident that, in the end, right living and right doing - ·must triumph.

IV

The Sculptured Figures *of* Society

VER the great doorway of one of New York's sky-scraping office buildings three colossal sculptured figures are posed in crouching attitudes. With their great bowed heads, grimly tense features, and muscles strained like whip-cords they seem to hold on their broad shoulders the terrific weight of twenty or more stories of solid masonry. They are really only—pompous shams. Theirs is only a Herculean pose. Theirs is only the pretense of the strenuous—not its reality. They were put in after the building was completed ; they could be removed without endangering the safety of the edifice in the slightest. They have no more real responsibility than a wandering fly, tarrying for a moment on the flag-pole on the roof.

There are thousands of such sculptured figures in the world of society to-day. They are men whose powers are evidenced in ounces, whose pretense is proclaimed in tons. They are those whose promises out-soar the eagles, whose performance is lower than the flight of the mud-lark. They are constantly posing physically, mentally, morally, socially, or spiritually. By juggling with excuses of their vanity and selfishness they may mislead themselves and others for a time but usually —they deceive only themselves. They are most often like the village fool who thought he played the organ when he only—pumped the bellows.

Certain fairly harmless sculptured figures have the pose of being "extremely busy." They constantly seek to raise themselves to a conspicuous ledge by the derrick of their own conceit. They seem to have so much to accomplish that you might infer that were each day two weeks long and three weeks wide, it would be absurdly inadequate for their diurnal duties. Their tasks are so " terrifically many " that, if you were optimistic enough to accept their statements as net, without asking for discount, you would realize that these tasks could never be accomplished by any individual—it would surely require a syndicate.

They belong to a class who, if they receive three letters in a day, tell you that they are "just deluged with correspondence." Their social engagements

are " positively tiresome " and as you
listen to the list of their society friends
your commercial instinct makes you
picture what a splendid élite directory it
would be were it only put into print.
Their troubles with their servants seem
so great that you wonder why they do
not discharge nine or so of them and
worry along with the remainder. They
use a seventy horse-power vocabulary
for a bicycle set of thoughts. They go
round polishing their own halos.

Another of these sculptured figures
poses as an intellectual Atlas holding
up the whole firmament of thought—
merely one world is too easy. His
ignorance and his impudence ever col-
laborate with his iconoclasm. He
demolishes literary reputation with the
ease of a sharp-shooter hitting glass
balls. He confides to you that Shake-

speare is greatly overrated, Thackeray was only a cynic, Scott a garrulous old novelist, George Eliot a sawdust doll, Dickens a tedious reporter. All the world's greatest dramatists, novelists, poets, philosophers and thinkers, are, one by one, inevitably bowled into —nothingness.

There is a sculptured figure who speaks as though pronouncing the last word of finality on science and higher thought. The problems that have baffled the sages for ages seem to him as luminant as an electric sign on a dark street. Though he has read, perhaps, partially through one volume of Spencer, Tyndall, Huxley, or Darwin, he erupts, like a pretensive Vesuvius of knowledge on—evolution. There are thick clouds of the smoke of mere words, and sputterings of confused light. Every weak spot in theology is known to him and where he cannot find a puncture he makes one. He seems to believe he could handle all cannon-ball problems as lightly as though they were rubber balls. Ignorance of many of these great questions is justifiable and natural to us who are not omniscient. It needs no apology, because one may be thinking honestly on other subjects nearer and dearer to one's life. The wrong and folly lie only in—the pose and the pretense.

There are other sculptured figures more sad to think of, more serious to contemplate, more blighting on the lives of others. They are those who peril the crown of their individuality by a moral or a religious pose—a combination of pharisaism, pride, policy and pretense. They may occupy high places but, like statues in cathedrals, despite the religious atmosphere and the environment in which they exist, they remain—only stone.

Religion to be worth aught must transform and sweeten and better lives or—it is only a self-deceiving formula. It must be a living impetus making them bear bravely their own burdens; it must broaden their shoulders to stand the strain of others' needs; it must make them active, virile, aggressive, inspiring powers in the world. Religion, to be really worth while, should, by their living, fill men's hearts with love, truth, right, justice, sweetness, honesty, faith, charity, trust and peace. These virtues can no more be kept hid from the world around them than can the blazing sun, riding royally in the zenith at noonday.

There are religious sculptured figures from sheer hypocrisy, consciously trading on their church rating—these may deceive the world without blindfolding their own eyes for a moment. There is a more subtle form where the individual himself does not realize that he is only an eye-servant or an ear-servant, that his is lip service only. He has no realization that he is not transforming what he believes is true into a dynamic moral force affecting his own life and the lives of others.

There are sculptured figures of friendship that may deceive us for a time. Discovery may take from us, for a long period, all that is best in us, shrivel our faith in humanity, and leave us lonely—until we bury the dead body of the friendship and learn to forget.

There are friendships upon the certainty of which we have staked our life. We have felt that though the winds of adversity might blow bleakly about us; the ships of our highest hopes wreck at the moment we believed they were almost in their haven of return; the night of our great misfortune settle down on us, without a star; the cup of sorrow, shame and suffering be close-pressed to our lips, yet despite all that might possibly come to us, there would ever be—this true friend by our side.

We may have shared his crust of trial and disappointment, heart-gladdened, in a way, that we were privileged thus to be of service to him. We may have listened untiringly to his endless repetition of the litany of some sorrow of his—soothing him, sweetly consoling, silently and sympathetically

comforting—with no thought of self.
We may have secretly left the death-
bed of some great hope of our own,
stifled our sobs bravely that he might
not know, and sat down with serene
patience to watch and nurse with him
at the sick-bed of some grief of his or
to help him towards the resurrection
of some hope of his from the grave of
his sorrow or his failure.

All that was ours, all the resources
of our whole life were more truly his
than ours because his need would stim-
ulate us to higher effort in his behalf
than we would make in our own. He
may have protested undying gratitude,
told us freely, over and over again,
that no demand or need of ours would .
seem even a drop to the ever-flowing
spring of his gratitude.

Then when the finger of time had

moved from days to weeks, and to months, the angel of a great grief may have knocked at the door of our heart, and perforce we have to open and let the angel of sorrow come in.   In the awful desolation and loneliness that numb our very soul we may turn round confident of meeting responsive eyes looking inspiration into ours ; we involuntarily bend the ear to hear words of courage from the lips of the only one in all the world that could comfort or console.   We reach out, by some subtle instinct, the hand of our pain, expecting it to be warmly covered but instead, we touch only—the cold, hard, chiselled outlines of a sculptured figure.

Then we realize the fullness of one of the most pathetic. cries in all the world's history, when Christ in the garden of Gethsemane, in sublime hunger of heart, in divine protest of soul, broke in on the slumber of Peter, with the words: "Could ye not watch with Me one hour?" We have faced a new tragedy of the soul—alone. The sculptured figure may never realize what he has done.

Real, honest effort, no matter how slight seem results, no matter how weak seem the progress, has no time for mere parade. Their high motives that inspire are: love, honour, truth, justice or those others that lead the ranks of their high purpose. The glowing realization that their work is serious inspires them. Their consecrated effort to rise to the heights of their highest nature—gives a royal importance that banishes trivialities.

True importance is always simple. The large duties, cares, and responsibilities of those seeking to do great things give them natural dignity and ease. They have the simple grace of the burden-bearers of India, who carry heavy loads on their heads and, in the carrying learn how to carry them, erect —with fearless step. There is in them no trace of the—pose of the strenuous. Men of serious effort think too much of their work to think much of themselves. Their great interest, enthusiasm, and absorption in their world of fine accomplishment eclipse all littleness. They are living their life,—not playing a part. They are burning incense at the shrine of a great purpose, —not to their own vanity. They ever have poise,—not pose.

The Hungers *of* Life

UNGER is the voice of a void. It is Nature demanding her rights. It is the restless insistent cry of an instinct, clamouring to be satisfied. There are four great hungers of life,—body-hunger, mind-hunger, heart-hunger and soul-hunger. They are all real ; all need recognition ; all need feeding.

The claim of a hungry body has right of way over all other needs. It requires no credentials, no argument, no advocate. It holds a first mortgage on the sympathy and aid of humanity. But the hunger for food while being most irrepressible, most immediately compelling, has no monopoly on the hungers of life. In the world to-day there are in reality more people starving for love than for bread. There is more heart-hunger than body-hunger —more unsatisfied yearning for sympathy, affection, companionship, kindness, and appreciation than for food.

These hungers are not a modern invention. They are as old as history. They began in the Garden of Eden. When Adam's bodily hunger was recognized and great stores of growing food insured him against starvation, the hunger of his heart was appeased by a wife. Then the mind-hunger of this first married couple was appealed to under the pretense that they should know the difference between good and evil. There was a soul-hunger still to

be met. They had the promise that
they would " be as gods."   There was
no evil in the four hungers but merely
that two of these were appealed to by
lying and treachery.   The wrong goods
were delivered—that is all.

We have all these four hungers be-
cause we are human—because we are
higher than the animals.   These hun-
gers are aspirations and were meant to
be satisfied.   They mean man's true
expression—not false repression.   Life
is a continuous battle for our hungers.

True living means realizing the real
hungers of ourselves and others and
seeking to satisfy them.   False living
means vainly humouring morbid ac-
quired appetites.   At Thanksgiving-
tide and at the Christmas season the
cup of our gratitude and kindness
specially overflows to others.   Let us

at this time, and at all others, realize that feeding the body-hungry is simply an initial duty. It is a first privilege of human brotherhood, good enough as a beginning but not as a full story.

Let us give others not merely what we *have* but what we *are*. Let us feed their higher hungers, not on set days and occasions, but in unbroken years of such days. Let us make this spirit —like a persistent, pervading perfume of inspiration—ever sweeten our own lives and those of others.

Mind-hunger is a craving for intellectual food. It may be an insatiable desire for education. It may reveal itself in a passion for books, in securing a few shelves of certain books for one's very own. It may mean the joy of possession of not mere books but of just those selected volumes that mean

silent friends talking ever inspiration
to one's eyes instead of to one's ears.
This is what makes a package of old
magazines or old books a treasure in
some lonely home after they have out-
lived their usefulness elsewhere.

This mind-hunger may be keen and
on edge for fine music, the hearing of
which would be a stimulus at the time
and later a golden memory ; while to
many of the box-holders it is merely a
social duty, a bit of a pose and some-
thing to talk about.   The mind-hungry
may long to have the privilege of hear-
ing a certain great lecturer, or, some-
times, there is a rushing wave of desire
to speak freely, fully, frankly to some
one who seems to live on the intel-
lectual heights, and to feed on his
words that if actually given personally,
in quickening advice or inspiration,

would bring real joy. These are but suggestions of the mind's hunger for that which it needs and craves.

The great heart-hunger of humanity is—loneliness. Loneliness is the heart's realization that no one is self-sufficient, no one is complete alone. It is always the restless yearning, in some form, for God's greatest gift to man—love. We seek it ever, consciously or unconsciously, as the great gnarled roots of trees, guided by some divine instinct, ever reach out in their constant search for the water that means life to them. The hungers for friends, sympathy, appreciation, confidence, companionship are simply phases, degrees, or tendencies of hunger for the finest human love—love of one alone for us alone.

In a great city there are countless thousands of men and women leading

lives of loneliness ; they are just heart-
hungry for the affection they feel is
their due and their right. It is not the
burden of daily toil, the smallness of
the reward, the dull round of daily
duties that make them heart-weary,
but that benumbing sense of loneliness
that sometimes sweeps over the soul
like a mighty tide and submerges every
thought but of—hunger for affection.

They just feel hungry for some one to
whom they can tell the little incidents
that make up their days, some one to
be genuinely interested, some one to
share their little joys and sorrows, some
one to smooth away the lines of care
and worry, some one whose eyes will
brighten at their approach, some one to
whom they will be necessary, some one
who will fill their sky with the sun-
shine of love and the glow of trust and

confidence. They want—some one to live for, some one to work for, some one to need them.

It is not always clearly formulated or even clearly understood, for the heart's feeling is often beyond its power to express. It may be only a vague, restless unsatisfiedness, but all the energies and emotions of the heart silently sweep themselves in one direction, as rivers, unknowing why, seek the ocean. And, with this heart-hunger satisfied, the magic hand of Time seems to have changed suddenly the whole perspective of life. The harsh outlines of cares and troubles seem softened and transformed, as the moon throws a glorifying silver light of interpretation over even the most prosaic of scenes.

When this heart-hunger is unappeased we may take cocaines of distraction that dull the pain they do not remove. We do a thousand little things to kill the time that hangs heavy on our hands, but this is not true living. It is the dullness of drugged emotion that keeps us from our best selves. It does not bring true peace; it is only—numbness. Real peace comes from finding oneself—temporary oblivion from losing oneself.

This heart-hunger is so real that it is not limited to those leading lives of real loneliness. It finds itself in homes where there is the semblance of real companionship, but not its actuality,— its cold, bare anatomy, not its living, pulsing, vitalizing soul.

There is a divine paradox in feeding the heart-hungry. As we seek to appease the heart-hunger of another our own grows less. The food increases in the using, as at the miraculous feeding of the four thousand at the sermon in the wilderness—what remained after all were fed was more than the original supply.   Let us make others forget *their* heart-hunger in the kindness, thoughtfulness, consideration, sympathy, companionship, and affection we can give them.   Let us forget *our own* heart-hunger in feeding others, even though we can silence ours in no other way.   No one occupies so humble a position that he cannot thus help.

There are times in the life of all when, weak and worn with the struggle, the ebb-tide of hope seems to carry out with it all inspiration, all impulse, all incentive.   In the darkest night of a great loss, a paralyzing pain, or a voiceless grief we seem to lose our very bearings on life, and weak, trembling hands

hold the useless compass of our pur-
pose. We see nothing to live for, and
life does not then seem worth liv-
ing. At such an hour gentle words of
comfort and courage and companion-
ship—words that come glowing from
the very soul of another, not empty,
cheap commonplaces that roll flippantly
from the tongue—come as living food
to the hungry heart.

When the trials of the individual
life seem hard to bear and the failures of
our best efforts tempt us to overthrow
the altars of our ideals, and all that we
have held high and best seems empty
delusion, we feel this hunger for a lov-
ing friend, a counsellor, a guide. We
want fresh, kindly eyes of those who
really care to look at our problems, to
help us to regain our faith in hu-
manity, our belief in ourselves, our trust

in the certainty of the final triumph of right, love, justice and truth.

To feed the heart-hungry we must give the positives of our life, not the negations. We must give our strength, not our weakness ; our certainties, not our fears ; our radiant finalities of decision, not our unsettled dilemmas.

If we were to transform " feed the hungry " from a mere phrase into a vital impulse finding expression in every day of our living, we would bring the very spirit of the millennium into the expanding circle of our individual life and influence. We would realize that these hungers are real and were given to man that they might be satisfied. They are not to be confused with mere morbid appetites, counterfeit hungers—man-made out of the idle hours of his folly. These must be

killed—starved into submission, domi-
nated, mastered, vanquished by the
individual who would be true to his
—kingship over himself.

Soul-hunger has its infinite phases
as well as heart-hunger. Soul-hunger
is man's insatiate desire to know the
truth of the life now and the life here-
after. Soul-hunger has existed in man
since the beginning of time. All the
religions of the world are simply sys-
tems to feed this spiritual hunger.
Hunger is the consciousness of incom-
pleteness. The belief in immortality,
another world, a new life, is simply the
—last great hunger of the soul.

VI

Throwing Away Our Happiness

F in the desert, a lone traveller, in angry protest against the hardships of his journey, were to slash with his knife his goatskin water-bag, letting the hot sand drink up the water that means health, strength, life itself, it would seem—supreme folly.

If a shipwrecked sailor were to slip voluntarily from his rude raft of spars in mid-ocean, thrust it far from him in disgust that it were not a finely upholstered boat, and, forsaking it, trust himself alone to the powers of winds and waves and darkness, it would seem —contempt for the mercies left him.

If we were to see a man idly roll a hundred-dollar bill into a splint, hold a lighted match to it and watch the charred fragments fall to the floor as a dead memorial of uselessness,—we would remember it for a lifetime. We would tell the story many times in the years to come. We would dilate on the waste, the folly, the great possibilities for good and helpfulness wantonly sacrificed to vanity and vandalism.

In our every-day life there are countless instances of happiness thrown away just as foolishly for a trifle,— perhaps but the puny gratification of a moment. It seems more hopelessly inexcusable than to cast aside a pearl and save the empty useless oyster shell that enclosed the treasure.

Our happiness rarely dies a natural death. We slay it with our own hand or others kill it for us. The veriest trifle may keep it alive, the veriest trifle may kill it, and yet selfishly, blindly, we still the heart of our own happiness or that of others. We may even irreverently throw the blame on the scheme of the universe—when we alone are at fault.

Happiness does not consist of what we *have* but what we *are;* not in our possessions but in our attitude towards them. It is the serenity of the soul in the presence of a present joy. It is not absolute, requiring certain fixed conditions; it is relative. What would be a fast for one might prove a royal feast for another. Happiness does not always require success, prosperity or attainment. It is often the joy of hopeful struggle, consecration of purpose and energy to some good end. Real happiness ever has its root in unselfishness—its blossom in love of some kind. We make or mar our own happiness and that of others to a larger degree than we are willing to admit. It is easier to pose as victim of conditions than to prove oneself victor.

The soul of our happiness may be —love. This love may be so fine and great and simple and it so fills our life that it leaves no room for pain, as light crowds out darkness. It may, with its Midas touch, turn even our trials and troubles into the gold of sweetness, strength and consolation. It may stand ever between us and the world—as a bulwark keeps back the sea. It may become to us an angel of hope holding our hand with gentle pressure when the clouds hang low, sustaining us when the way of life seems hard.

This honest love may ever trust us; forgiving and forgetting may be its atmosphere. It may inspire us, recreate us, give wings to us when downcast, a new shield to faith and new heart to energy. We may have this great happiness all our own, firm in our grasp, yet for a mere trifle—we may throw it away, or let it fall gradually from us— like pearls dropping, one by one, silent and unnoted, from a broken necklace.

We let some petty, mean trait of ours, some weakness we should master through self-control, cheat us of our happiness. We have held some penny of momentary satisfaction so close to our eyes that it eclipses the sun of our happiness. A foolish jealousy that deadened our ears to explanation, that shut our eyes to the truth and that stilled our tongue when it would speak the words of faith we could hardly keep back—we have let this jealousy, this snap judgment, expressive not of real love but of wounded pride, swallow up our happiness—as the ocean engulfs a treasure-ship.

We may let idle gossip, false sympathy, imbecile advice from those who know absolutely nothing about our real condition, shut us from love and faith, breed doubt and suspicion, and choke trust as by the fumes of some noxious gas. We may let some other folly which comes from our false interpretation cheat us of our happiness like one ignorant of the meaning of a deed —signing away a fortune.

And when it is all over we may not have the moral courage to go back, as we should. When later, conscience holds in a bitter hour of realization and loneliness its sad post-mortem over the dead happiness, it may be a very poor satisfaction to know that we killed a love that we needed and that needed us—for such a trifle.

Friendship that meant much in our happiness, that was rest, refuge and joy, may be thrown away for a trifle. Friends, real friends, are rare in the individual life. We cannot have many of them. They do not come in bunches like bananas. They are never found ready-made at all. They are formed by weathering the same gales of fate together, by standing the heat of conflict together, by kinship of mind and heart, by common interest in a common ideal, by basic understanding, mutual dependence, thorough respect and loyalty that grows stronger as need grows greater. Acquaintances we may

have many, but acquaintanceship is—
merely the grapes of possibility from
which the rich wine of friendship is
aged and mellowed.

Friends are usually necessary to
happiness. Robinson Crusoe could
hardly have been genuinely happy
in his isolation, no matter how he
kept his optimism breathing by fre-
quent applications of oxygen from the
tank of his philosophy. Even love
does not long satisfy unless there is
in it real friendship and companion-
ship. Love is, in reality, only a
supreme, unique brand of perfected
friendship. But we may throw this
element in happiness away in a mood
of selfishness or blindness.

For the empty pleasure of a clever,
cutting taunt we may give a stab-
thrust that may kill a friendship. We

may take the kindly expressions of our friend as a matter of course, demanding as a right what belongs to us as a courtesy. You cannot force a spontaneity any more than you can make the bud a full-blown rose by forcibly opening its petals. The bud becomes a rose by natural expansion from within. A friend's need is our opportunity. A momentary neglect or coolness at a psychologic moment, when the tired heart needs sympathy, encouragement or help to the utmost, may begin the death of a friendship.

Some people like the dividends on friendship, but not its assessments. They really do not need a friend, they want a bank. When there is not mutual helpfulness—not necessarily the same in kind or in degree, but the helpfulness in which each gives freely his best to the other as naturally as a flower exhales perfume—the friendship is like a patent that is nearing its time of expiration.

Ingratitude kills friendship or rapidly attenuates it to a point where it must die of anæmia. If we value our happiness or our friend, let us gladly expend the time, energy and thought required to keep the relationship—free, clear, fresh-running as a mountain brook. An idle flippant breach of confidence, at a moment when it seemed almost calculated treachery, may kill a friendship or a happiness growing for years.

A hasty surrender to temper, a sudden heat of anger may be followed by a drop of sixty degrees in the temperature of a relation between two people. It may destroy a real happiness as a blizzard may, in a single night, ruin a fruit field. There may be an unkind letter, a cruel fling of cynicism or an unjust slur or sneer that meant only venting our own sad disappointment, chagrin, or deferred hope, on an innocent friend. We may have been conscious of the injustice before the words were cold on our lips but some mean streak in our nature may have kept us from calling them back.

We are often happy in our hopes, our plans, our purposes or our possessions and let the envy of another poison the well-spring of our happiness. Envy is a drug that stupefies energy. It does not give us what seems so beautiful to us merely because it belongs to another. The very thing we desire might not fit us nor agree with us even if we could get it. Have you ever noticed how much more interesting your neighbour's paper looks than your own, as you let your eye wander to what your seat-mate is reading? Have you ever felt that the meal some one else has ordered looks much more appetizing than yours, even though you could have had precisely the same if you had desired?

Happiness does not come from comparison of our lives with others; we have our own life to live at its best, not—the lives of others. Let us get what we can from our own paper, our own meal, our own life. Let us live so intently, so bounteously that the joy from our life will overflow into others, will make us better able to help others, will transform us into castles of refuge to those who need us.

Nursing a grievance does not bring

happiness. Being hypersensitive to the opinions others have of us puts us into the false position of making their approval our court of appeals instead of our own conscience and self-respect. False pride too often betrays us into surrendering the realities of life for the poor satisfaction of an hour. Some persons are so busy putting poultices on their wounded vanity that they let their happiness die of inanition. Living each day at our best, simply, sincerely, sweetly, is the surest way to win happiness and—to hold it.

VII

At the Turn *of* the Road

N walking along a mountain road there is sometimes a sudden sharp turn where, by seeming magic, the narrow path is transformed into the entrance of a vast panorama of Nature. We seem stunned as we involuntarily stop short, rest and surrender to its majesty. The view exalts us, glorifies us, inspires us. We have a new high restful ground of contemplation. We have a new test of values, a new base of interpretation, a new relation to life.

The hamlets and villages in the valley bear a new strange dignity—they have become integral parts of a great picture. The colours of trees and flowers blend from mere single effects into a wondrous harmony. We are seeing the birth, life and death of a river as an eagle might watch it from his nest on the crags. The fields of a hundred farmers become one great farm. And far beyond, we can see the great ocean—whitening the shore with its billows leagues away.

The complex has become simple the absolute has now become relative; the isolated has become associated; the trifling great, and the great greater the detail losing none of its individuality has an added value like a jewel set in a crown. There is a finer sense of justice in our judgment, the ozone of the higher levels seems tonic to our soul, a sweet peace fills our heart.

As we look backward the narrow path, doled out to us in installments as our weary feet toiled up the long ascent, now stands out clear—for its entire length. We begin to see it as a type of our whole life, as the angels must view it with greater charity from the higher wisdom of their truer perspective. Rest, retrospection, reflection, realization, and revelation are giving us a fine new view-point, a new chance to get our moral bearings, to tune our life to bring out its highest, purest notes—at the turn of the road.

Humanity tends to take narrow views of life and its problems instead of occasional great, broad sweeps. It is near-sightedness of the soul that permits the unworthy to throw the really big things into the shadow. We hold some trifle of care or worry close to our vision as a jeweler with an awning over his eye peers into a watch. We let one sorrow be the grave of many joys, one ingratitude smother many of our kindnesses struggling for expression, one weakness within us sap the strength from many virtues. We need the bracing inspiration, the revealing illumination of the larger vision. The turn of the road, in its highest sense, is not a place to stay—we have to fight the battle of life. It is only an arsenal of supply—not a battle-field of action.

The beginning of the new year is a natural, sharp turn in the road of time. Here we may wisely rest a while, and in the peace and quiet and calm of self-communion see the long stretch of the road of a single twelvemonth. It is built imperishably of short steps of living—from moment to moment.

Many of the purposes for which we laboured and struggled, in our narrow, close, selfish absorption, seem poor, petty and puny when seen from the turn of the road. The structure of some effort we thought marble now is shown in its sickening sham as a hasty affair of show and pretense, made of staff, that could not stand the wear and tear and test of time. It was not built on square lines of character, of the best that was in us. It lacked strength, sincerity, simplicity. The material was made up of policy and selfishness put together on hurried plans. It was a failure; it cannot be rebuilt; but it is worth only a passing regret and a realization of the lesson of its non-success—at the turn of the road.

We now see how many times the paralyzing hand of procrastination touched the good deeds we meant to do, the roseate dreams we longed to transform into actualities. We wished to do and we wanted to do but we did not *will* to do. The fault was not in conditions but in—us. We were not equal to opportunities. It is a false philosophy that teaches that opportunity calls only once at any man's house. It comes with the persistency of an importunate creditor, always in a new guise, and clamours for admission, but we may be—too busy to answer the bell.

Habits that we had determined to master, to bring into sweet harmony with our highest self, may still stalk large and insolent before us. They may seem to taunt us that they are stronger than we. They were never made in a day and cannot be mastered in a day. An hour may begin the making of a habit; an hour may begin its breaking. Time, with heart and mind united in determination, can conquer any evil habit or create and confirm any good one.

The look backward from the turn of the road should inspire us by making vivid to us how much of what we feared never came to pass. The tyranny of worry, that dominated us and held us for months trembling slaves to a weak fear, that dissipated our energy, dulled our thinking, and darkened our mental vision, at the very hours that should have given us fullest control of our best, is now seen as an enemy to true individual growth. It means a harder fight in the unending battle against worry and grief.

The broader view of life reveals that

the only great things in life are trifles; that what pained us most, saddened our hearts, and turned our hopes to ashes were only trifles—cumulating into overwhelming importance. A cruel word, an unkindness, a little misunderstanding may darken a day and separate us from one we love or may petrify us into a mood of doubt and despair. The most joyous moments of life, the high lights in the pictures of memory, may too be only trifles of kindness, fine expressions of love, simple tributes of confidence and trust that make the very heart smile —as we remember.

Knowing the right is useless unless —we practice it. Realizing our weakness is profitless unless—we seek to change. We may even grow so comfortably reconciled to faults and fail-

ings as to accept them as finalities, to
confess them and even boast about
them. It is unjust to ourselves and
unjust to others. Some people treat
their faults as though they were flaws
in the Portland vase of a noble nature
and as if—pointing them out were
practically banishing them forever.

Nature is constantly giving us new
—turns of the road. It may be a
birthday or some general anniversary
in the cycle of the year. It may be
some red-letter day in the private cal-
endar of our emotions or some date
eloquent to us as telling of some joy-
ous "first" or some pathetic "last"
time in the sacred diary of the heart.
It may be a supreme sorrow, an ago-
nizing sense of loss, the coming of a
great joy, the closing of some epoch in
our lives, the proving of the actuality

of something too awful for us even to have feared, some exultant half-hour that changes irrevocably all our living. These and numberless other days, hours or single moments may bring us alone to—the turn of the road.

Then may come one of those rare moments of life, of fine spiritual discernment, of luminous revelation, of coming to one's highest self, when the sordid, the mean, the temporary, the selfish are stripped in an instant of their garish shams and tinsel. Then the real, the true, the eternal stand out in their majesty, bathed in the splendour and glow of the revealing of truth. In such a spirit the very tingle of the inspiration of the infinite fills us. We seem born again to new, better, and greater things, for we have seen the divine vision—at the turn of the road.

VIII

Sitting in the Seat *of* Judgment

LINDFOLDED; holding
in her left hand a bal-
ance; in her right a
sword—thus they pic-
ture the goddess of Jus-
tice. This is satire in symbolism. It
seems the work of some cunning cynic
concentrating in a single figure the
worst elements of human *injustice* and
grimly labelling it "Justice." It is
worse than a label—it is a libel. This
goddess of Justice has her eyes deliber-
ately closed to the facts. She holds
ostentatiously on high the scales of
justice but never sees their movement.
She has her hand tight-pressed on the

sword of punishment before even hearing the testimony. She is excluding all evidence but one—hearsay.

This is the goddess of Justice that dominates society to-day. The true Justice should be open-minded, open-eyed, open-eared, open-lipped, open-handed. Serene, free, unhampered by bonds without or by prejudice within, she should have one object—to discover the truth. Nothing should escape her searching vision; no faintest whisper elude her eager ears; with finest honest wisdom should she question, and with free unencumbered hands investigate, test, prove. The lamp of truth should throw its dazzling glow of illumination on every trifle of evidence. The balance of judgment should be held rigidly on a support before her, not suspended from—a trembling arm. This seems a higher and truer symbol than—a blind woman, sporting her regalia.

Character is not a simple, uniform product. It cannot be judged as dress-goods—by a yard or so of sample unrolled from a bolt on the counter. It is complex, confused, uncertain, changing, subject to moods that contradict our conclusions. While knowing all this we dare to construct the whole life and character of one we may have never even met. We build it from a few hints, slurs, idle comments, or the vague rumours or absolute lies of newspaper reports—as scientists reconstruct an unknown prehistoric animal from a few bones. One judges a painting by the full view of the whole canvas; separate isolated square inches of colour are meaningless. Yet we dare to judge our fellow man by single acts and words, misleading glimpses, and deceptive moments of special strain. From these we magnify a mood into a character and an episode into a life.

There is entirely too much human judging, too much flippant criticism of the acts of others. Suspicion is permitted to displace evidence, cheap shrewdness to banish charity, prejudice to masquerade as judgment. We imagine, we guess, we speculate—then pass on through the medium of indiscreet speech and idle gossip what may bring bitterness, sorrow, heartache, and injustice to others. The very ones we condemn may be battling nobly under a hail of trial and temptation where we might fall faint in the trenches or, lowering our colours, drop back in hopeless surrender.

We have a right to our preferences,

our likes and dislikes, our impressions, our opinions, but we should withhold final judgment—as an honest unprejudiced juryman keeps his verdict in suspense until he has heard and tested all of the evidence. We have no right to let prejudice tyrannize over judgment and kill—the justice of the soul. We may see an act but have no luminous revelation of the motive behind it.

We idly condemn the gaiety of some man who has suffered a terrible loss, and term him heartless. Perhaps he laughs only to keep back tears that would gush like a torrent from his heart were he less brave. We criticise the parsimony of some one when it really means consecrated generosity to some one else. Over-generous forgiving may seem weakness—when it is the " ninety times nine " of a great nature. Love at its height may seem indifference. What appears conceit may be only some one's attempt to recover a lost self-confidence he hungers to regain.

Some one's fretfulness, or occasional outbursts of temper, may be but sparks of protest from the hidden fires of a sad life-story or some bravely borne illness unknown but to a chosen few. Meanness may in reality be poverty too proud to confess itself. We hear one side of many a story and judge by that alone. We judge often along the line of our least mental resistance. Ignorantly we condemn a man for vanity because we would be vain had we accomplished his work. There is wide difference between putting yourself in another's place and putting him in yours. The one is an attempt at wisdom ; the other a speculation in prejudice. We misinterpret motives, do not know facts, and judge from wrong standards.

In the individual life we realize that there are times when everything we do or say misrepresents us. We mean kindness but somehow the words sound cross, cruel or misleading. Without intending it we hurt those who are dearest; we regret it, know the sad effect we are creating, yet we blunder on into deeper pitfalls. We may be even too falsely proud to explain. We are all out of key. We are tobogganing down the incline of a mood. We may not understand ourselves and in a spirit of heart-hunger may long for some one sweetly and gently to comprehend us, to see us truly, despite —ourselves and our acts.

Knowing this labyrinthic quality in us and even in human nature at its best, let us throw the golden mantle of love and kindness and justice over every thought of condemnation. How can we judge others harshly when we do not know ourselves and while we suffer so much from the misjudging from others? Let us live in the open sunlight of love, shutting our eyes in charity from adverse judging—just forgetting much, forgiving much.

Let us sweetly, sincerely, sympathetically seek in the best side of some one we know—his real, fine, true self. Let us think of the fine flowers and ignore the weeds as temporary invaders. This may prove an inspiration to some one near and dear to us to live up to our ideal of him, to be worthy of the higher levels to which our faith has raised him.

Sometimes situations arise between

friends that demand rapid judgment and action.   Then should we check off the items carefully, considering truly both sides of the ledger of our experience.   Before pronouncing sentence let us see if in our heart of hearts we honestly believe our verdict fair, just and true.   Let us be assured it is justice—not prejudice, pique, temper, disappointment, distorted gossip, or aught else that is eclipsing the justice of our judgment.   Our injustice, if such there be, may change bitterly the life of both.

One of the hardest lessons of life is to learn not to judge.   Perhaps ninety per cent. of the adverse criticism, comment, and judging of humanity is unnecessary and serves no useful purpose. It is not our business.   It is simply our mere impertinent meddling in the affairs of others, without even a hope of being helpful or useful. It is often what we would most quickly resent —were the situations reversed.

There are times in every life when we *must* judge, when we should judge, and when it is vitally important that we should judge wisely and justly. There are those closely associated with us in love, friendship or business— where it may be important for us to understand their words, their acts, their motives, and their emotions in so far as they affect ours. The very attitude of not judging until it becomes necessary gives ever dignity, calmness, poise, and fineness to these enforced judgments. The judgment that has been dulled by constant misuse, like a razor that has been used to sharpen pencils, is of little value in real need.

The wisest judgment means the best head cooperating with the best heart. It is kind, honest, charitable—seeking truth, not the verifying of a prejudice. It says ever, in prefacing its conclusions on the evidence: " As it seems to me," " If I understand it aright," "So far as I have been able to reason it," " Unless I am mistaken," or similar phrases. These represent the suspended judgment—with no tone of absolute finality. They show a willingness to modify the verdict, to soften the sentence, or to order a new trial if new evidence, new illumination, or new interpretation can be produced.

Only through sympathy can character be rightly understood. Intolerance and prejudice poison judgment. Even our worst enemies are not as bad as we think them. When Apelles, the Greek painter, made a portrait of Alexander, King of Macedon, he painted the monarch with his finger on a scar received in battle so that the disfigurement was not evident.   Let us not point out the scars on the lives and characters of those around us but let the kindly finger of charity gently obscure them.

To kill the judgment habit where it is unnecessary, we must silence expression, but we must do more—we must learn not to *think* severe judgment even if not spoken.   If we do judge severely in our thought it colours our acts and our attitude.   When tempted to judge let us ask—" Is it necessary ? " When hearing gossip let us ask—" What are your proofs?"   We should stifle our own criticisms and silence those of others.   In judging others let us have courage to say, not coldly and uncaring but from the depths of human love and sympathy—"I really cannot tell.   I do not know."

There is an Oriental legend that one day, Christ, wandering through the streets of Jerusalem, came suddenly on an idle crowd of jeerers over the dead body of a dog.   Each spoke contemptuously, each condemning some phase, each contributing some meanness to add to the cruel merriment.   Christ stood silent for a moment, and then, pointing to the open mouth of the dead dog, said—" Ah, but no pearls are whiter than his teeth."   This spirit of seeking ever the best side in our daily living would absolutely transform it.

IX

The Inspiration *of* Possibilities

HE world needs the clarion call of a great inspiration on the unmeasured possibilities of the individual. No man that ever lived exhausted his possibilities. The greatest that ever shed the glory of their presence on this earth of ours have given but at most a few-sided showing of the lines upon which they concentrated. None ever lived the full, rounded, perfect flowering of his whole nature—the vastness of his possibility remained in the silence and secrecy of the unexpressed. Life is too short for the full story.

The feeling of the incompleteness of this life, its unsatisfiedness, is a strong base of belief in—immortality.

Let us throw overboard that benumbing philosophy of the words " Remember your limitations " and preach ever : " Remember your limitless possibilities." With the new dignity added to the individual life comes a finer realization of the power of maximum living from day to day, a large, firmer grip on individual problems. There will be a revelation that must tend to kill shams and pretense. There will be a truer attunement with the highest real things in life. There will not be the folly—the disheartening " limitation " adage so fears—of people attempting to succeed at once in lines where only genius or years of consecrated effort can hope to achieve.

Man is not put into the world as a music-box mechanically set with a certain fixed number of tunes, but as a violin with infinite possibilities. This music no one can bring forth but the individual himself. He is placed into life not a finality, but a beginning; not a manufactured article, but raw material; not a statue, but an unhewn stone ready alike for the firm chisel of defined purpose or the subtle attrition of circumstances and conditions.

It is only what a man makes of himself that really counts. He must disinfect his mind from that weakening thought that he has an absolutely predetermined capacity like a freight-car with its weight and tonnage painted on the side. He is growing, expansive, unlimited, self-adjusting to increased responsibility, progressively able for large duties and higher possibilities as he realizes them and lives up to them.

Man should feel this sense of the limitless—physically, mentally, morally, spiritually.   Newspaper and magazine stories of men who came to this country with seventy-six cents and now own thirty million dollars and head a trust tell the financial side of possibility.   It is here deemed unnecessary to give *new* appetizers for a national hunger—so well developed.

From the physical side man may realize as a removed "limitation" that some of the strongest, most healthy and athletic men were weaklings in childhood and even young manhood.   They made themselves anew by exercise, outdoor life, sunshine, simple food and adherence to the laws of health which constitute the common sense of Nature.

There is no loss of any of the senses nor of limbs that has proved a handicap fatal to success of those great ones who had cultivated a fine contempt for obstacles that dared to daunt them.

The possibilities of mental development stand vindicated in the splendid roster of the great ones of the world who with smallest opportunities of education, fought their way to the ranks of great thinkers, men of rare individuality, and real leaders in the world's advance guard to the higher things. Never were books so cheap or so accessible as to-day and but a trifle of time consecrated daily to this development would work wonders for him who not merely wishes and wants but *wills* to realize possibilities.

No one in life occupies a position so humble, be it in the smallest hamlet or the largest city, that he cannot manifest his moral strength and exercise it. There is none so obscure that he cannot make the lives of those around him marvellously changed, brightened and inspired if he would merely progressively live up to his expanding possibilities in the way of kindness, thoughtfulness, cheer, good-will, influence and optimism.

Better far is it for the individual to be a live coal, radiating light and heat for a day, than to be an icicle for a century. It is better to be an oasis of freshness and inspiration, if the oasis be no larger even than a table-cloth, than a desert of dreariness— larger than the Sahara. We can all be intensive, even if we cannot yet be extensive; deep, if we cannot be wide; concentrated, if we cannot be diffused.

The smallest pool of water can mirror the sun; it does not require an ocean. Let us live up to our possibilities for a single day, and we will not have to die to get to heaven; we will be making heaven for ourselves and for others right here—to-day on this little spinning globe we call the earth.

What a man *is* at any moment of life does not fix what he may *become*. It is not necessarily a destination; it may be merely a station; a chapter, not the complete story. Progress is but the continuous revelation of possibilities transformed into realities. We see the running, but not the goal. It is not results that are the true test of living, for they may lie outside the individual's power to control, but it is ever the moral and mental qualities he puts into the struggle. The world's standard of judging is not in accord with the higher ethics of the soul. It is not getting the best, but proving worthy of the best, that is the revelation of true character.

The man who talks airily of the things he would do if only he had time, unconscious of the golden hours of wasted opportunity frittering idly through his fingers, had better wake up. He often envies those who have performed some marvel in self-education, when but a small section of the time he squanders in a year with the lavish recklessness of a Monte Cristo would enable him to learn a new language. Every hour is a new chariot of time's possibilities that might be laden with rich treasure, but if man tacks up the sign " no freight," he should not complain of the subsequent barrenness of result. The roll of the great leaders in human thought and effort have *not* been those who had the best opportunities, but those who made —the best use of them.

There are men battling with the soil on poor, anemic farms, that yield but a bare living, while underneath those acres may be rich veins of coal, wells of oil, that need but the revealing, or beds of other minerals that mean liberation from the slavery of poverty. It is not easy to make them manifest, but the greater treasures of the individual's possibilities within his own heart, mind and life he *can* bring out if he only will. Self-confidence is a virtue that should never lead a single life; it should be wedded—to tireless energy.

There come high-tide moments in all lives when contemplating some heroic deed, when our ears are filled with the triumphal music of a great thought, when the vitalizing words of some great thinker or teacher reach our soul through our eyes with a message of illumination. We then see our life in new perspective. The meanness and emptiness of living on low levels shame the soul out of self-complacency, and we seem to see wondrous visions of our possibilities, glimpses of what we might become. It is a coming face to face with our higher self that may re-create our lives for all the years if we only will. Let us realize our progressive possibilities, make them real, vital, growing, not uselessly held—as a warm living seed may rest for years in the dead hand of a mummy. Realizing possibilities is the soul of optimism, and optimism is the soul of living.

X

Forgetting *as a* Fine Art

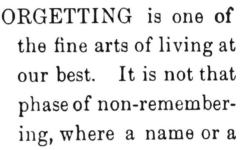

ORGETTING is one of the fine arts of living at our best. It is not that phase of non-remembering, where a name or a date or a fact has not strength enough to keep itself from sinking deep into memory's sea of oblivion. Fine forgetting means character asserting itself— not mind losing itself. It is the blue pencil of wisdom—cutting out unnecessary words from the text of our living. It is individual kingship determining what thoughts it will permit to reside in its kingdom. It is the exclusion act of the soul—ejecting the unworthy and the undesirable. A great editor once said : " The true secret of editing is to know what to put into the waste-basket." Forgetting is the soul's place for losing discarded thoughts, depressing memories, mean ambitions, false standards, and low ideals.

All the virtues, vices, and qualities of mental and moral life may be defined in terms of—forgetting or of remembering. Selfishness is forgetting others in over-remembering self. Worry is the inability to forget the troubles that may never happen. Honour is remembered high standards made evident in acts. Anger is the explosion of an over-heated memory. Forgiveness is the heart's forgetfulness of an injury. Ingratitude is the heart's forgetfulness of a favour. Habit is the memory of acts making repetition easier. Mercy is the memory of human weakness tempering justice. Envy is forgetting one's own possessions in over-remembering those of others. Influence is the remembered acts of one inspiring the acts of others. Patience is forgetting petty troubles along the way in concentrating thought on the goal. Love is the heart's sweetest memories shrined in another.

Forgetting as a fine art has two distinct phases: learning how to forget and what to forget. Forgetting is the heart's eclipse of a memory. It is so easy to say lightly to some one suffering from a memory, " Oh, just forget it all." Those of us who have sought honestly and bravely to fight it out on the silent battle-field of the soul know that forgetting is never easy. If it *were* easy there would be neither credit, courage nor strength in mastering it.

Those people who tell you moral battles are easy, really know nothing about it, care nothing or they are getting ready to tell you they have just remembered an appointment and must say " good-bye." It is a real fight but we can win in the end—if we are not afraid of a quick, hard fight. It is better than a long siege of remembering that lasts for years.

Keeping the world from knowing our pain or struggle by veiling our sorrow with a smile, seeming to forget, is fairly easy ; but this is not—real forgetting. The biggest souls find it hardest to forget. Trained forgetting is paradoxic. We cannot forget by *trying* intensely to forget—this merely deepens and gives new vitality to the memory. True forgetting really means finer memory ; it is displacing one memory by another, by a stronger one, an antidotal one. It means concentrating on the second phase so that the first is weakened, neutralized, and faded out like a well-treated ink-stain. It is removing a weed from the garden of thought and then planting a live, sturdy flower in its stead. It is cultivating new interests, new relations, new activities. Time helps wonderfully, but especially when we go into partnership with her.

If we learn to forget wisely and unselfishly in the trifles of our daily living with others, we shall silently accumulate higher pressure reserve power for our own later needs. Let us forget thorns of daily living in remembering roses of its possibility; forget things that pain in remembering unnoted reasons for thankfulness; forget the

weakness of those around us in seek-
ing to discover wherein they are strong.
Let us forget the disappointments in
the courage of new determination ; for-
get the little wrong we have suffered
from our friend, in living again in
the memory of his many kindnesses ;
forget the things that depress in con-
centrating on those that exalt.   Fine
forgetting is an attempt at—finer jus-
tice.   It means aggressive living—on
the uplands of truth and light.

The man who lets the really great
things of life, love, honour, duty, trust,
friendship, loyalty, justice, selfishly
slip away from him for the mere grati-
fications of a moment or a mood, has
no right at first to forget.   His first
duty is to see that he has not been
keeping his conscience under the ether
of self-apology.   He must realize the

wrong and do all in his power to right it. Then in his new strength the petty things will lose their treacherous charm. They will fade into the dim recesses of forgetfulness where they belong, and the real things will stand out again strong, luminant, inspiring.

There are moments when a man rejoices that he is living, that he is yet able to do the right thing he disdained—to fill some one's life with roses, clear some one's path of sorrow. He has the new opportunity of doing a big man's work in a great simple self-forgetful way.

He who listens gleefully to scandal, turns it over meltingly on the tongue of appreciation, and then syndicates it with supplementary chapters of his own guessing, repeats it until it becomes a stained tattoo in memory. His ears should be debarred from listening and his mind taught to forget by thinking deeply of the pain such scandal would give to him, were he or some one dear to him the victim, innocent or guilty.

He whose success has made him hard, selfish, intolerant, and critical, who has no patience with those who have not succeeded, should rest for a little from his work of pinning new medals on the chest of his self-approval. He should forget his unworthy vanity by recalling his own hard struggles and the part that chance, patronage, favour, or even questionable cleverness, has had in incubating his prosperity. He may then gladly extend the helping hand he now withholds.

We often let an act of the long ago poison our present living : we remember when we should forget. There are

things done in the inexperience of
youth, in moments of unreason, acts of
many years ago, that have left livid
scars in thought, that sting and canker,
that discourage and deaden purpose, de-
press our moral vitality, dim our men-
tal vision, and dull our energy. We
should let the dead past bury its dead.
We should put them forever out of life
and thinking. If we have made all
reparation possible, let us consider
them as the acts of some one else—a
weaker self that is now dead, not the
self that lives to-day, the one we are
seeking to make finer and better. Let
us make our new self more than a
monument to a dead past. Let it be to
us a prophetic tablet to the greater self
we are preparing.

Remember and think of past folly,
mistakes, sin and sorrow only long

enough to repair, to atone, and to avoid. Then forget the yesterdays of sadness, shame, wrong, and failure in the soul's concentration on the new, fresh, clean days for higher, truer living, making each new to-day but the prelude to a new, better to-morrow.

It was this fine forgetting Saint Paul meant when he said, " Forgetting the things which are behind, I press forward to the mark of my high calling." Forgetting of this type is simply—forgiving ourselves for past errors. We forgive others for wrongs where there is true regret, realization, and the promise, direct or implied, of non-repetition. If we are honest in our determination, if we really have acquired new wisdom, why should we not thus forgive—ourselves?

Forgetting is the hardest lesson of

life, and it is never so hard as with the memories of the emotions. Our bitterest moments of living are when we drape our sweetest memories in black because they belong to a past that is dead forever. There are high-lights of remembered joy that overcome us with maddening pain, harder to bear than any actual sorrow, past or present. There are memory cells that we long to identify, to individualize and to isolate from the millions of their fellows in the brain and to kill—as the electric needle deadens the life of an individual hair-cell.

"Sorrow's crown of sorrows," says Tennyson, "is remembering happier things." Long, hard sorrow is a sickness of the soul, from which in time we may gradually emerge. Nature gently leads us back to health in our days of emotional convalescence by helping us to forget and by giving us new memories to remember. Memory is a mental force we cannot kill; but we can direct, we can give it new subjects to act upon, new right engines of purpose to move, new channels into which to run.

There are sometimes petty fractures of our pride, irritating incidents that hurt perhaps because we are nervous. They loom large before us. For the time each seems as big as a real sorrow or loss. If we cannot master it may be as well to surrender to it just for a little, to think it out, to talk it out, to get it out as much as possible from the emotional system. *Then* we should cease to think and to talk; we should learn to forget, avoiding situations and conditions that revive the pain, seeking right work and association that lead from it. Then even a great cankering sorrow will be conquered. If found unworthy we shall find it silenced forever in our hearts and—dead in our memory.

Let us seek to begin each new day in the consciousness of our crown of individuality as serene and calm as though it was a new life, with nothing of the old remaining but its wisdom, its sweet memories, its duties, its responsibilities, and the hope, joys, privileges, love, and possessions the old life has bequeathed to us.

The Victoria Cross *of* Happiness

APPINESS does not come from folding our hands serenely, filling our hearts with the minor music of resignation, and gazing heavenward as though posing for a spiritual photograph. Happiness is activity, not torpor; doing, not dreaming; finding oneself, not losing oneself; illumination, not illusion; reality, not imagination. Happiness does not fool itself by believing that whatever is is best; it seeks constantly to find whatever is best in what is and—tries to make it better.

Making ourselves believe we are

happy by thinking that we are, is a poor brand of self-hypnotism. It does not bring happiness, any more than imagining we are dining sets before us a table with a real, eatable dinner of nine courses. Constantly declaring loudly we are happy when, in the deep indigo of a mood, we feel that happiness is for us forever as extinct as the dodo, is not brave ; it is dishonest. It is playing a confidence game on the credulity of our friends. It is false optimism—the voice of the pessimist lying about his troubles. True happiness does not brag—it radiates.

If the trials and sorrows of life depress, one should not deny but realize them and then instantly seek to change conditions, as the engineer stops his train at a danger signal and aids in removing the obstacle on the track. If our sorrows be real, we should then bear them as bravely as we can by concentrating the thought on brighter things. We often accentuate our pains by hot poultices of self-sympathy that we constantly apply to our wounds. We do not let Nature gently heal them; we do not seek to forget ours in helping others to forget theirs. Delusion never gives reality. Reality comes only from truth—right thinking followed by right living.

The Infinite gives to no man happiness; but only the raw material from which it can be made. He provides iron ore but never plowshares, clay but not bricks, wheat but not loaves. The material from which one man forms only an abode of misery, another transforms into a temple of joy. Happiness is a manufactured article; it cannot be bought or sold, it must be home-made —by the individual himself. The only man for whom a ready-made Paradise was provided was Adam— and he spoiled it all and was evicted. All the other people have had to make their own paradises or go without.

Life is not a summer holiday, or a personally conducted tour through joy-land, or a dream we must accept just as it comes—it is a struggle, a battle. We must do our part; we must fight, —fight, too, with no war maps of the full campaign spread out before us for our consultation and inspiration. We must fight the enemy that is nearest, vanquish the duty that stands in our way, help the faint and fallen, win every point of higher, better, clearer vision, be ready for whatever comes— with a true soldier's defiance of the

odds against him.   Whatever is worth
while is worth the fight to attain it.
If you want happiness, fight for it like
a man.   Fight to be worthy of it, fight
to win it, fight to keep it, fight to share
it, fight to help others get theirs.

Fighting for happiness is paradoxic.
We must battle for something higher
than happiness or we will not win it.
He who aims at it directly always misses
it.   He gets a poor, weak, adulterated
brand of selfishness that proves that
his satisfaction, pleasure or joy is only
a flavoured cheap substitute.   Nature's
pure food brand, the real article, never
has a bad after-taste, it never palls.   He
who is living on the higher levels, bat-
tling bravely to be at his best, placing
happiness secondary to love, right,
honour, ideals, truth, unselfishness and
justice is the one to whom it comes.

Happiness is the moral Victoria Cross of life. It is an *extra* award given for kingship over self, a fine victory on the battle-field of self, " for valour," for the good of others.

More than fifty years ago England established the Victoria Cross—that simple Maltese cross of bronze with a decoration and the words " For Valour," the whole suspended from a ribbon. It was given to soldiers, sailors, and to all others who proved worthy by special acts of unselfish bravery in imperative need.

Of the thousands awarded this most highly-prized honour few, if any, ever thought of it for an instant at the very hour—they proved supremely worthy of it. Thrilled with sublime courage in the heat of battle they over-rode mere duty by a higher inspiration.   Love for humanity made some rise to supreme heights of daring to save the lives of others.   Some stood, brave and undaunted, fearless, almost blind to every danger in the hour of supreme need of a nation, an army or an individual.

Forgetting self, forgetting the fearful hazard, forgetting the spellbound spectators, forgetting all but the imperative call for instant action, their plan was hardly conceived before its accomplishment was begun.   They responded to some divine impulse that so filled the human that it left no room for thought of the Cross.   They forgot it but they proved worthy of it—and later it was pinned on their breast.   Let Happiness be our Victoria Cross—given because of our proving worthy.

The battle-field in our fight for hap-

piness is not the world but—self.
Mere attainment of wealth, fame, suc-
cess, position, power, or possession does
not necessarily bring—happiness. The
history of the ages proves this. Hap-
piness comes ever from within. It is
the atmosphere of an inner calm and
peace. We must battle not for hap-
piness directly but—against the ele-
ments within us that keep happiness
from us and valiantly on the side of
those that will help us win it. There
are traits within us that often poison
the cup of happiness when it is safe
within our hand,—jealousy, malice,
stubbornness, envy, pride, selfishness,
idleness, fear, worry, suspicion, and a
host of others. Let us realize the ele-
ments that keep us from happiness,
keep the need of mastering them before
us, and we start bravely on the road.

Worry is a common enemy to happiness. It is restless surrender to vague fears, not meeting them singly, but multiplying them. It is the insistent, irritating iteration of one disturbing thought. Have you ever struck repeatedly one key of a typewriter when the ribbon does not move and then found it worn through in a few moments? There is no progress, no writing produced, no result but useless wear. This is how worry acts on the mind; it eats through energy, purpose, vitality, and produces—nothing. It is not the sunshine of clear thinking focused on a problem; it is a dull, distorting, blurring mental fog that creates phantoms where none exist. It is not easy to control; but it can be conquered, and it must be or it will darken the whole life of the individual. Taking shorter views of our daily living helps greatly.

Living from day to day, making each day a complete life in itself, doing each day our best, and in the realization we have done our best facing results bravely,—this is the magic formula that somehow we must learn to transform into real living. Worry has a corner on most of the—unhappiness in this life of ours.

We must fight against selfishness if we would win—happiness. All the sins, weaknesses, and follies of human nature are simply selfishness appearing and reappearing under a hundred disguises or changes of garb. Selfishness is treacherous because it produces a temporary counterfeit of happiness that cheats the individual. It gives a semblance while destroying the reality. It puts him out of touch with humanity, kills his genuine interest in others, isolates him, intensifies his demands while diminishing his real resources, destroys his true perspective of life, builds up a false self-sufficiency, a self-finality. Nothing that lives in nature lives for itself alone. The plant that absorbs what is to it life-food, carbonic acid from the air, must exhale oxygen or it will die. Giving is as vital as getting. Fighting for happiness means getting it in order that we may give it, and by giving it we get it again in new form.

Nothing outside man can make him really—happy. It must in some way enter into the very fibers and substance of our lives and thought and needs. Happiness ultimately means self-conquest, self-harmony. It is the higher self ruling in peace over a conquered lower self, as a victorious general wisely rules a city he has taken. Happiness must not be confused with content, satisfaction, comfort, pleasure, and joy. These are but sparks, while happiness is the electric atmosphere of the heart, —living, pulsing, glowing. It is the gladness of the soul that inspires and strengthens the individual to face conditions he cannot change.

Happiness does not mean living under skies of perpetual sunshine, where pain, sorrow, sickness, longing, trial, failure, and poverty are forever banished. They can never be banished from the world. But the positive, brave, aggressive spirit that inspires us in the fight for true happiness is greater, deeper, stronger, and higher than these. It dominates them when

they come, as a sturdy swimmer over-
comes the threatening surge. It re-
duces the frictions of life, transforms
their bitterness into sweetness, their
pangs into power.

The great invaders of human happi-
ness are not the great trials and sor-
rows, but the treason of petty day-by-
day unnecessary worries, wrongs, and
injustices manufactured by ourselves
or donated to us by those around us.
Fighting for happiness lessens these in
number and in force. Love gives us
that quick instinct for finer vision in
seeing wondrous possibilities for hap-
piness for ourselves and others that no
mere reason of the mind could dis-
cover. Love is the instinct of the
heart. Purpose, a concentrated, conse-
crated object in living, helps to hap-
piness for ourselves and for others.

There is only one minute a day, when the sun is at its zenith, that it casts no shadow. At every other moment the stronger the sunlight the deeper the shadow. There are rare fleeting moments when the sun of our happiness is at its highest ; *then* there are no shadows. Let us see the sunlight in our life so strong and with so concentrated a determination that the shadows will hardly trouble us. Let us not put off the expectation of happiness to be realized in some great future, but find it from day to day in the trifles of life—as the children of Israel gathered, fresh every day, the manna that fed them.

XII

The Crimes *of* Respectability

RESPECTABILITY wears white robes of superiority and is vain of her virtues. Respectability keeps within the pale of human and social law though breaking the laws of—the finer code of the soul. With Pharisaic self-complacency she withdraws her dainty skirts from contact with crime. She sits serene and self-appointed in the seat of judgment and deals out hard condemnation on the offenders of human law—the criminals, the outcasts of society. Let respectability listen for a moment to the charges to be brought against her and then quietly, squarely and honestly face the issue and see its justice.

We must realize as an absolute fact that all the crimes of criminals in any city or state, massed together and awful as they may be, cause but a very small part of the suffering of life and affect but a small fraction of the people compared with—the crimes of respectability. Let us realize that it is from the regular army of respectability that life's greatest sorrow comes—not from the scattered skirmishers of crime. If we honestly accept and believe this truth, we have a new illumination, a high impulse, and a noble inspiration towards higher, simpler living.

Were we to question a thousand or a million men we would find that but a small percentage have ever had their lives darkened by deeds of crime, in fact, by any acts punishable by human law. But from the cruel, unnecessary, unpunishable weakness and injustice of every-day life—none is ever long immune. The crimes of respectability are gossip, jealousy, envy, bitter words, hypocrisy, scandal, malice, persistent meannesses and injustice, lying, temper, hard, uncharitable judgment, selfishness, spite, ingratitude, treachery, and —a host of others.

Gossip is one of the popular crimes that has caused infinitely more sorrow in life than—murder. It is drunkenness of the tongue ; it is assassination of reputations. It runs the cowardly gamut from mere ignorant, impertinent intrusion into the lives of others to malicious slander. If facts do not exist it creates them. If the facts be innocent it somehow juggles them into evidence of black guilt. In interpretation it always chooses the worse of two possible motives. It constitutes itself a secret court of inquisition that decides on the fate of the victim in his absence—when he has no chance to speak in his own behalf. It is a conspiracy of wrong.

He who listens to this crime of respectability without protest is as evil as he who speaks. One strong, manly voice of protest, of appeal to justice, of calling halt in the name of charity—could fumigate a room from gossip as a clear, sharp winter wind kills a pestilence. Sometimes gossip does not deal altogether in words; there are simple yet subtle tricks of silence and gesture—and in a moment the deed is accomplished. It seems like a whiff from one of those diabolically poisoned roses of the Borgias that kill and leave no sign. Then a reputation lies dead in the roadway. Some one's mighty faith in some one has its pulse stilled forever. Some one is walking his weary way alone in the silence with the sun of love blotted from his sky.

There is satanic ingenuity in quoting part of a sentence and without telling why or how it was spoken. It puts a man of honour in a position where he cannot explain because he knows not the treason. This seems the master-stroke of gossip. It may kill a great love in an instant and leave no chance for explanation that might drive out the poison of a lack of faith—unjustified were the truth known. The happiness of two may be killed by—this lying silence.

Jealousy has a hundred masquerades

in which to do its deadly work. In countless business enterprises alone it transforms the joy of honest faithful service into a grim inferno of hopeless struggle. Inferiority, incompetency, or selfish, impotent ambition is seeking to undermine the best efforts of others. By tale bearing, petty intrigue, trickery, imposition and all those other small implements of warfare that make up the armoury of small minds they seek to harm others. The venom of jealousy, self-distilled, poisons not only others but their own whole natures. They envy but do not emulate. If the constant energy expended in injuring others were concentrated in heroic efforts to better themselves the results would be vastly different for—themselves and the world.

There are men who wear the white

badge of respectability as jauntily as
though it were a fresh white pink in
their buttonhole.   They like the favour
of the community as expressed to them
by smiles, cheery words, and pleasant
greetings on the morning walk to the
station.   They may show a different
side to their families.   They may have
irritability, impatience and a waspish,
mean temper that upsets a household
day after day.   They leave a long trail
of bitter memories and of rankling in-
justice, that runs from the breakfast
table to even-tide.   They vent their
temper on their family and on inferior
employees who cannot resent it—never
on a business customer or associate.
Prudence, policy and politeness forbid.
They are thoroughly conscious of the
limit—they rarely play it.

When the master returns the mem-

bers of the family look up question-
ingly to size up his mood as a farmer
surveys the clouds to determine what
the weather will be. The sorrow caused
by professionals who steal tangible
things is microscopic in comparison
with the misery caused by respectable
amateurs who rob their homes and
offices of happiness—by temper alone.

There are women in some communi-
ties with reputations that are spotless,
—as the world's standard goes. Their
uniform of respectability seems always
fresh from the laundry. Those who
know them best know they are narrow
and bigoted, hard and uncharitable in
their judgments, unforgiving, selfish
and bitter. Their very influence is
blighting; they are daily transforming
some one's Eden into a desert. They
shrivel generous impulses of those

around them. They pass through life, self-mesmerized by their selfishness, in sublime unconsciousness that they are doing more real harm in the world than some whose acts they regard with profound horror. Real human love seems as dead in their hearts, as destitute of the slightest light or warmth or glow as the centuries-old ashes of Pompeii. These women are not necessarily hypocritic. They are only taking a Rip Van Winkle sleep of selfish self-satisfaction. No one seems to have the courage to waken them—with a strong dose of straight talk.

The daily evils that make life hard are not the great sorrows from which under the healing touch of time we may rise sweetened, softened, strengthened, facing life bravely anew. They are the infinity of irritating trifles, the cruelly unnecessary injustice, the absolutely man-made wrongs of life. It is irreverent to refer to them as any part of the divine plan. These wrongs are as much man-made as—a pair of shoes or a watch or an automobile.

There is selfishness that overrides the rights of others like a car of Juggernaut. There is a bitterness of unforgiving condemnation that listens to no reasons, explanations, or motives, that believes because it has seen, that credits the senses and accepts circumstantial evidence as final. There is avarice that starves what it should feed. There is ingratitude that, turning traitor to the kindness it has received, dries for years some generous fountain of giving. There is hypocrisy that, masquerading like the devil in a surplice, poisons love and friendship and leaves scars in memory and sears and warps character. These are a few of the crimes of respectability.

A large part of the evils in life is preventible ; some by the individual— alone. Why do we not prevent them ? Man longs to learn the secrets of the Infinite in this universe of His, as though it would change man's whole life. If man be not true to what he knows, he is not ready to know more. With many people it is like a child who, not yet having mastered his primer, is hungry for Shakespeare.

Man is said to have been made in the image of his—Creator. Some men seem to be trying—to remove the labels and other identifying brands. If we are *men*, with the dignity of our powers and privileges and possibilities, let us just—live like men. Life is not something to be lived through, it is to be lived up to—in all its highest meanings and messages. There was in the army of Alexander the Great a soldier, who, although he bore the very name of the great conqueror, was in his heart a coward. Cowardice in any soldier of that mighty army was the worst of all crimes; yet for this man to be a coward was shame unspeakable. And Alexander in great anger commanded the craven: "Either give up my name or follow my example." Living up to our privileges means living up to our name—anything less means failure.

If for a single week in any city each individual were to say each morning: "To-day no one in the world shall have even one second darkened by any act of mine," and live it—that city would be transformed and glorified.

It would, after all, mean only *negative goodness*. It would mean only the avoidance of evil, not real, aggressive, positive, high-keyed living at our best, but the burden of life would be lifted, the heavens would almost open and be visible. Then in an atmosphere warm with the radiant glow of love and brotherhood we could almost hear the faint rustle of the angels' wings—the angels of peace ushering in the millennium on this world of ours.

XIII

The Optimism that Really Counts

OPTIMISM is the sunshine of the soul radiated in action. It is true religion as a living, compelling fact—not a mere theory. It is sturdy confidence that right must triumph—united to tireless courage to make it triumph. Optimism is the finest weapon in the armoury of the individual. It unifies all the aggressive undaunted virtues of his strength into a force and an inspiration. It means fighting for, or with, the battalions of right, love, justice and truth—with determination to win. True optimism is something more than a continuous performance of hope. It is the joy of living—made an actual fact. It means seeking the best, living the best, doing the best. It means focusing all that is highest in our character to meet conditions.

Merely thinking, hoping and trusting that somehow, somewhere, somewhen, things will come out right while we do nothing to make them come out right is sunstruck folly—not optimism. It is a hammock philosophy for a sultry day when you are too drowsy to think and really do not care what whimsey of non-thinking plays games in your mind. No farmer outside of the pages of " The Arabian Nights " would expect nature alone to seed and fertilize and plow his fields and then to harvest his crops and put them in his barns without any human help whatever but his thinking. The exaggerated belief in the superhuman effect of thought as a direct power, is—the folly of many.

This truly comfortable restfulness is merely a perfumed hot-air sentimentality. It dulls moral energy and deadens purpose. It is opiatism—not optimism. It is only mental or moral laziness wearing a rainbow robe of beautiful confidence. It may give a temporary fictitious strength to character but is ever revealed as weakness—in a crisis. It is only a papier-maché shield—punctured in the first battle with the stern realities of life.

There is a light, jaunty, bubbling, care-free humour that takes the low fences of petty worries—neatly, gracefully. It smiles nonchalantly because it has never seen real trouble. This light-weight philosophy usually wilts at the first touch of real sorrow, grief and loss, like a straw hat meeting a sudden rain-storm. This is a sort of kindergarten optimism that sees only the sun—untouched by clouds. Real optimism knows the sun is ever shining —despite the dark, heavy clouds that may obscure it. It knows that darkness is ever the herald and messenger of dawn—the new illumination and inspiration that must come. True optimism seeks to live in the broad sunlight—when it can. It seeks to rest serene and confident of the outcome —when all seems dark.

Verestchagin, the great Russian painter, had a glass studio constructed at his home near Paris. It revolved on wheels, moved by a windlass placed near his easel, and he was thus enabled to paint all day with the sunlight falling

—in one direction on his models and drapery. He who has cultivated optimism to be part of the real equipment of character thus turns constantly to the light of truth, love and kindness and to the growing brightness of the *real* things of our living.

Cheerfulness has done much good; it has been stimulating, kindly and helpful. It causes a cheery message. It often prevents sorrow, worry, deep grief from becoming contagious. This cheerfulness is sweet when natural; brave, strong, and sturdy when assumed. Cheerfulness is a sort of germicide of the emotions; it deadens their power to injure others and soothes the individual. But cheerfulness at its very best and highest is not—optimism. It has never the full, free completeness, finality, depth of—optimism.

Cheerfulness may be a blossom of which optimism is the plant. Cheerfulness may be refreshing rills of which optimism is the fountain. Cheerfulness may be a smile on the face; optimism is the smile in the heart—when one is fighting hardest. Cheerfulness may be the gentle, bubbling voice of a hopeful temperament or a sunny disposition; optimism is the clear convincing, individual tone of the finest depths of our character.

Optimism seeks to discover the good points in the acts of those around us, to let their little weaknesses and failings fade into nothingness in the shadow of our charity. It seeks to emphasize their best, to recognize it, to appeal to it, to call it forth and to develop it. A smile, a word of sympathy, a touch of human kindness, a hand-clasp of fellowship, an unexpected bit of tenderness, courtesy or consideration will accomplish wonders. It is syndicating sunlight and that is what real optimism is. It has a cheering magic healthful power that no amount of criticism or reproof could accomplish in changing others. True optimism must begin in the—thought. It must be real and living in word, act, and atmosphere. It cannot be put on as a veneer from the outside; this is a grand-stand play, not a private performance.

Optimism cannot foresee the suffering that may come to us, but we can sturdily determine the effect we will let it have on us. Sorrow comes in so many guises but we must all "drink our cup." The hardest of all our cups of sorrow comes from the hand that should never be the one to force it to

our lips, or it is some cup that gives
agony to us because we cannot save
another from it.   There is the stirrup-
cup of parting, when we turn our
horse's head away from the inn of our
hope—never to return.   The quassia
cup made bitter by that from which it
is cut and more bitter in memory.

The loving-cup, when moistened by
unmeaning lips and passed to us, may
later seem to carry a note of treachery
we may not understand aright—till
too late.   There is the cup of consola-
tion that kindly hands gently press to
fevered lips.   There is that greatest
cup of a final supreme grief like that
given to the great Optimist of Calvary
that " could not pass."   These are but
types of the cups of life.   We should
drink them—if drink we must—as
Socrates bravely drank his poisoned

hemlock, valiantly quitting a world unworthy his noble life with them.

The man of optimism should be kindest in criticizing others and never put the hand of harsh judgment on the unhealed wound of another's sorrow. Keenly, vividly, personally conscious of the trials, cares, sorrow, hunger, loneliness and suffering of life, he knows how often he failed and still fought on till at last he found his way —back to the sunlight. The optimist believes courageously that there is a reserve strength in man that brings sudden new inspiration to bear or to conquer, like the unexpected arrival of new food or troops in a siege.

The optimist, with new courage in his heart, new determination in his mind, and rebel tears secretly gleaming near his eyes, may rise superior to all

unjust assaults. He may accept need-
less pain without cynicism, may meet
betrayal without thought of revenge,
may have to battle face to face with
cruel disappointment without flinching
and yet be victorious in a bettered self
though vanquished in what was dear-
est—the hope and heaven of his living.

Optimism realizes that life is bigger
than any single battle. The true soul
has no final Waterloo; it has only its
latest defeat, with its golden message
of why it failed and how it may win in
the next conflict. There may be in a
very defeat an unnoted victory within
our own life—a new revelation of
latent power, and a glow and tingle
of new courage. This may come to us
while the bugle notes of triumph of the
enemy still ring in our ears, their
flaunting shouts of victory yet telling

us of the prize we have lost and their
smiles of conquest hardly faded from
their eyes and lips. Many a seeming
defeat may force us to retreat to higher
grounds, where we may stand in
stronger array, reintrenched, rein-
spired—to fight harder than ever.

With true optimism, we can face
poverty without permitting it to
harden us, we can meet trial and sor-
row and remain calm and unworried,
stand bravely when we do not see the
way to walk. We can let the glow of
optimism so warm our soul that we re-
main simple, strong, sincere, and un-
ruffled despite any environment. We
thus may conquer adverse conditions
by making them powerless to harm us
—when we are unable to change them.
Optimism is the armour of brave souls
who fight conditions and never sur-

render to domination by the darker side of life that dares to daunt them.

The optimism that counts does not let the individual—take whatever thoughts may come. It is a power that enables him to a degree to select his own thoughts, to stimulate and encourage those that add to his strength, that are wings to his purpose, that thrill his energy with new consciousness of power. He gains control over those memories that take the smile from his face, strength from his mind and joy from his heart. Optimism inspires a man to reduce all depressing effects to a minimum, to raise resistance to a maximum, to cut off the friction of worry and useless regret. They magnify weakness, minify strength. Optimism has no use for them.

We never make conditions easier by

telling ourselves how awful our troubles are; by feeding our griefs for fear they may die a natural death; by intensifying every element of pain. The optimism that is worth anything makes one person smile at troubles that would put another out of the running altogether. It finds joy because it is trained to see the tiniest glint of it as a miner's eyes are quick to recognize the slightest speck of gold in his pan. Optimism sees roses in life because it is looking for them; receives love because it is exhaling it. It forgets its sorrows in counting anew its blessing. It makes life truer, higher and finer for self by making it sunnier for others. This is—the optimism that counts.

XIV

Power of Individual Purpose

URPOSE gives a new impulse, a new impetus, a new interpretation to living. Purpose is the backbone of a life of courage. It shows that the highest justification for living is love —in some form. It may be for a cause, a country, an ideal, a family, or an individual. Purpose at its best means our kingship over conditions, our mastery over self, our dedication to something higher than self, fighting for the right and fighting it to the end. Were we able to follow even a great purpose from its highest flights of

effort we might find its nest of inspiration—in the heart of some one of whom the world knew nothing.

Purpose makes man his own second creator and by it he can make himself largely what he will. He can choose his own realm: he can live contentedly in the mud of low desires like a lizard or sweep boldly high in the pure, inspiring, bracing air of noble ideals like an eagle rightfully claiming the mountain tops as its own.

If our aim be low, mean and selfish, bringing out all that is weakness in our nature, an ambition that betrays its method in the despicable things employed to attain it, it is unworthy of our crown of individuality.

Low purpose makes us experts in petty sophistries; it kills natural sweetness and kindness; it raises the moral temperature to a fever heat of "don't care" and lowers the vitality of all our higher living. This is not the purpose of which we speak ; it is individuality at a discount, not at a premium—as we should hold it.

Purpose makes man a crusader—for something. He seems to grow greater before our eyes in his efforts to reach and grasp the cross of some ideal— though it may seem to us unattainable —when the inspiration and glow of the struggle itself means more to him than even a crown of victory. Purpose is conscious, continuous concentration to attain an end. Before it can be greatest there must be union and unity— body, mind, heart and soul acting to· gether, as the essence of many flowers may be fused into a single perfume.

To many of us the eagles of purpose

of the world's exalted great ones may be impossible to us in our present conditions. We may be bound by duties, cares, burdens, the daily problem of mere living that make great deeds difficult. But we can all have purpose and should have it and we should live to it at its best. We must finally be judged not by attainments but by the ideals and motives that inspired them. There is one purpose that no one is too humble to live by. It is—"faithfulness in little things." It may be only a new impetus of loyalty, trustfulness and watchfulness in our daily duties.

Employers find great difficulty in getting this very faithfulness in little things. Many of those paid for service are only eye-servants. They are listless, lazy, and irritably languid—except when off duty. They regard the

repeated instructions as to how certain
simple work should be done with an
airy nonchalance that is indifferent, im-
pudent and impertinent. They forget
everything except some trifle of personal
interest; this is tattooed into their mem-
ory. They collapse under the slightest
strain of responsibility like an intoxi-
cated man leaning against an imaginary
post. They are a bundle of excuses—
where their own failures, foibles or
flaws are under discussion.

Workers such as these consider
merely getting a maximum pay-envel-
ope at a minimum expense of mental
or physical energy. They wonder why
some other worker is retained or pro-
moted while they are sure they have
worked just as long as she has each
day. They forget they have not
worked as wide or as deep—they over-

look these two other dimensions. It is
the *plus* of purpose consecrated to doing
daily one's best with a constantly added
increase of ability that makes the real
difference. This simple phase of pur-
pose may change the life of an individ-
ual and inspire ever higher purpose.

The conquest of a weakness in char-
acter, the acquirement of a new lan-
guage, a concentrated attempt to be of
greater usefulness to others in some
way, to prove equal to our possibilities
as they progressively grow larger under
attainment—these may be but purpose
in a small way. Purpose unites the
separate days of our living by the thread
of continuity—as scattered beads form
a necklace by the golden strand run-
ning through them. A mother may
make even the care of her home and
her family a *real* purpose if she puts

into her labours the best that is in her, ever realizing she has—her crown of individuality she must never forget.

Many men in this life, men of position, power, wealth and opportunity, are—merely drifting. They are not victors of their course but—victims of the current. They live but have no definite purpose in living. In easy-going, careless, free way they are carried along by the tides of life, with no self-consciousness that they are drifters. Some of them do no defined great evil but no real good. If they were to do some great evil or fall before some great sorrow or trial it might be the means of startling them into realization, shocking them into vivid consciousness of their lack of purpose. Man does not drift into goodness,—the chance port of an aimless voyage. He must fight ever for his destination, ready to battle, with calmness and constant courage, against fog, darkness, adverse winds, and dangers that should only inspire to greater effort.

There is hardly any peril of the sea more dreaded by mariners than a—derelict. It carries no lights on bow or stern, no passengers, no rudder, no pilot, no crew. It is bound nowhere, carrying no cargo, to no port. Helpless in itself it is a menace to all others. Human derelicts are those ignored as hopeless by others, but they were first deserted by themselves. Lack of definite real purpose is the royal road to drifting, desertion, and derelict.

In seeking material success it may be necessary to grasp a low rung of the ladder ; but on the ladder of purpose begin with the highest rung your out-

stretched hand can clasp and hold on
till you reach the next.   Purpose takes
man out of the orchestra of life and
puts him on the stage of real action.
It makes him part of the spectacle, not
a mere spectator.   It gives him a real
part to play, one no other could play,
in the great drama of humanity.

The great thing in life is not in real-
izing a purpose, but in fighting for it.
If we feel the possibilities of a great
work looming large before us and im-
pelling us to action it is our duty to
consecrate ourselves to it.   Failure in a
great work is nobler than success in a
petty one that is beneath our maximum
of possibility.   We have nothing to
do with results—they do not belong
to us, anyway.   It is our duty to do
our best bravely and then to rest in the
comfort of this fact alone.   But be our

work great or small let us have real purpose in life and battle for it undaunted to the end.

Purpose at its best must be above and beyond us like the polar star that guides and inspires the compass of the mariner. The world needs, more than talent, genius, wealth, or power, men of simple, earnest purpose, men consecrated to daily living in the inspiring illumination of an ideal ; men who make each day count directly for something real, who face each day's sunset with new harvests of good for those around them and for the world.

Being good, merely good in a pale, anemic, temperamental way is not enough. If the world is not daily better because we have lived, if the little circle of those around is not brightened, strengthened, heartened, helped, and some way made happier by our direct effort in our conscious living, we are not true to purpose or possibilities. We cannot all be Lincolns and save a nation, but we can put the spirit of Lincoln into every trifle of our living —his simplicity, courage, kindness, love, consecration, justice.   The greatest good to the world is not the magnificent power of a few great men manifesting it on a colossal scale, but these same qualities, in a smaller, humbler way, manifested in millions of simple, unknown lives throughout the world.

XV

When We Forget the Equity

IFE simplifies wonderfully if we stand on a truer base of interpretation. We lose much of the real joy of living because of—our one-sided view. We accuse Nature of playing favourites. We imagine she is giving us all the hard benches, and to others, seemingly, reserved seats of preferred positions with an unnecessary supply of easy cushions. We may think Nature strews the path of one with roses while working overtime in collecting the thorns for us. It seems she sends us the great real sorrows and hands our

neighbours across the street only an occasional bon-bon trouble put up in a perfumed, beribboned box.

We forget we know only part of their trial or sorrow—never all. We forget while we know all our troubles, we do not recognize all the good we might enjoy if we would—the un-noted things dear in our lives that should greatly lessen our pain. We forget the equity.

In business the equity is the net value of a house or other property over all mortgages or claims against it. There is an equity in your favour, on a bookkeeping account, if what is owed you is more than what you owe.

Two men may have all their possessions in the separate ownership of two houses. The one who has a three thousand dollar house free from debt may envy the owner of the ten thousand house next door, unknowing it is covered by an eight thousand dollar mortgage leaving this man's equity at two thousand dollars. The owner of the small house is the richer of the two men. It is the equity that proves it. The philosophy of the equity illuminates many of life's greatest problems. It may soften the pain and sweeten our living by showing how equity intensifies our optimism. Recognition of the equity helps us to retain our crown of individuality.

Under the seeming injustice of life Nature is constantly seeking—equalizing, balance, justice. Nature keeps books with the individual. Her justice consists neither in the debit nor in the credit side of her ledger, but in the difference,—the net, the balance, the equity. What seems to us injustice is often really only our concentration on one side of the account—to the exclusion of the other. We exaggerate our sorrows so that they eclipse our joys. We are unjust to what we have in hungering for what we have not; we make our unsatisfied desires, not our possessions, the test of happiness.

Sometimes, with a sigh on our lips and a sob creeping into our throat, we face our life in numb rebellion. We are so vividly conscious of what we have to bear that we may forget our reason for happiness. Our sorrows, seen through the magnifying glass of discouragement, loom large before us. Our joys through the reducing glass of unsatisfied desire minify into almost— nothingness. We permit what we lack to poison the waters of what we have.

We forget the equity. We forget the big, clear, broad sweep of net happiness still remaining to us. The mortgage of care, sorrow, and responsibility blinds us to our *real* possessions.

There are times when some affliction, some illness holds us in its close deadly pressure. The pain seems beyond the bearing. It seems so unjust, so cruelly hard to suffer. It mars our life; disturbs the simple sweetness of the best in our nature; keeps us ever slaves under the awful spell of its presence or under the grim tyranny of fear of its recurrence. It makes us sometimes bitter and unjust in our poor misleading speech. But in our temporary times of relief the tide of courage, love, gentleness, tenderness runs just as strong as ever, just as earnest, in the high sea of our heart's desire.

If we can remember the equity we can make slightly easier this bed of pain. We may find joys in thought that lull the pang. We may find our place in life a little softened from the struggles of the past, some good fortune may add to our equity; the touch of some inspiring friendship may hearten us to new bravery. We may realize that, because of our very illness, in the windings of time, the craft of some great joy has sailed to us, along the river of sorrow, and anchored in our heart.

We may envy the fame, fortune, or prosperity of another, unknowing the mortgages of care, responsibility, opposition, and worry that reduce the realness of what he has. We might be unwilling to pay a small percentage of the price it has cost him. His net happiness may be really less than ours.

A business man may pass through fearful times of stress and storm, trying hard to keep the flag of hope ever flying, watching carefully for rocks of financial discredit, delayed payments and heroic effort—to bring his ship of enterprise safe into harbour. The employees, leaving at the stroke of the bell, may go home and drop all thought of business. They look with envy, perhaps, at his easy position, thinking and knowing nothing of his constant courageous battle. They like the property, forget his mortgages of worry and responsibility and overlook the sympathy and better work and loyalty they would give if they realized—the equity.

They who have no children feel they are the one thing lacking for happiness. Those who have them may concentrate on the hardship of so many to feed and care for and educate. One may put too much stress on the loss, the other too much on the responsibility. Both may forget the equity.

One great reason for much of our manufactured sorrow and misery is that we measure our lives by what we judge of others, not by true estimate of our own. Life in its highest sense is not a competition with others but with ourselves. Have you ever sat in the local train and felt you were making good time? Suddenly the express whizzes by, with a rush and a roar, in the same direction on a parallel track. As you watch this train your own seems not only making no progress whatever but seems actually going rapidly back on the track, nearer to its starting point. When the express disappears you become conscious that your train has really been cutting distance all the time.   Of course we realize it is only an illusion.   In our daily life we make similar mistakes that vitalize our sorrows and put happiness into a moaning restless sleep, with wet eyes at dawn, because we—forget the equity.

If we have really much to bear, our attitude is making the bearing harder. It is making our power over conditions less, their power over us more.   Let a fresh, clear, bracing breeze of optimism and new courage blow through the soul. Let us forget our sorrows in remembering our joys; lessen our pain in realization that our imagination is increasing it.   Let us remember the equity, the great possibilities, powers, and possessions for good to ourselves and the world—still left to us.   If even *then* it seems little, throw in great handfuls of hope, purpose, confidence, determination, courage. Let us make it seem greater—until it really becomes greater.

We are inclined to regard all happiness, success, and sunshine as our due, which we have earned somehow by merely coming into the world and consenting to live here, while—trial, sorrow and pain seem an unjust invasion of our individual rights. The possession that would be the crowning joy of one might be the useless encumbrance or the last stroke of despair to another. We forget the equity in judging ourselves; we forget it in judging others.

In our bookkeeping in business we do not let some one's debit of one hundred dollars wipe out his thousand-dollar credit; we realize that the man has an equity of nine hundred dollars remaining; that he has this amount still to his credit.   Why do we not let such justice apply to the acts of others?

The friend who has been kind and generous to us for years, who has stood bravely by us in hours of darkness, whose hand has steadied us through a crisis, who should have many golden spots in memory to his credit,—may prove weak, may offend us, may even desert us.   In our hurt we may let the act of a moment neutralize the years of constancy, truth, and loyalty,—one debit cancel in an instant his long account of credits.   We make it harder for him, harder for ourselves, by forgetting the equity, by overlooking the margin still remaining to his credit.   A little patience, a little tolerance, a little generous waiting and watching before pronouncing final judgment, may do wonders in this weary world.

For years some man in public life may have struggled by consecration to purpose, by loyalty to principle, by faithful adherence to duty, and at last —reached a pinnacle of fame. The world honours him ; his life is held up as a model, an inspiration to the young, a source of pride to all. But that man may do a wicked thing, and the world is startled by the discovery. Society says, " Now he is unmasked ; now we know his real character ! " One evil act becomes typical of a whole life. One evil act submerges all the good of years of faithful service.

Does society ever make one good act the expression of a character ? Does it ever let one good act sweep like a mighty tide over a wicked life and bury it forever from sight and memory ? That man's character may not have been hidden.   There may have been a sudden temptation, one that came when mind was weary, hope weak, and body worn, every sentinel against sin, for the time, withdrawn—and the victory was an easy one.   Under the compelling power of an act once committed, morally dazed, he may have involved himself further—doing what he could, not what he should.   The act was wrong. It was a big black mortgage on a life; but the equity, the justice of the balance of good, is his—and we wrong him by forgetting it.

Poets, preachers, teachers, delight to say character is a mighty structure, put together block by block, which may be ruined in an instant, fall into dust and chaos by one evil deed.   It is not so— this is cruelly unjust, untrue.   Character cannot be killed in an instant—it is only reputation that can be slain by one act. Great single deeds do not make character—large single evil acts cannot ruin it. Character is built of trifles. The real test is the equity,—the balance of the good over the evil.

It may be the Infinite will finally so judge us; that He will regard no single black act as being our whole life; that He will judge us by our equity, letting good impulses, high motives, faithfulness in little things, true unselfishness, brotherly love, kindness, and exalted ideals, balance, offset, and neutralize many of the acts of our human weakness, as we—in our poor human recognition of justice—permit a payment on account to cancel part of a debt.

is do not make

XVI

Running Away *from* Life

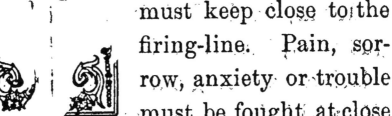

O fight life's battles one must keep close to the firing-line. Pain, sorrow, anxiety or trouble must be fought at close range. They cannot be evaded, ignored, nor deserted. We must vanquish them or they will vanquish us. We must look them squarely in the face and—fight them to a finish. Retreat means simply deferring the battle until we are weaker—not stronger. It is running away from self—running away from life. It is as foolish as trying to dodge the atmosphere.

Thousands in the world to-day are

running away from life to escape some
mental or emotional pang. They are
seeking it by the road of amusement,
distraction, travel and change of scene.
They seek not new wisdom to cure a
wound nor new strength to bear it, but
merely—some way to deaden the pain.
These are in quest not of peace but of
temporary oblivion —not self-conquest
but self-forgetfulness. They are taking
emotional cocaine, which, like all pow-
erful drugs, has a dangerous reaction.

The swiftest engine in the world
cannot carry us away from a grief that
holds our very heart in its close deaden-
ing pressure. No matter how rapidly
the mile-stones are whizzed backward,
we cannot escape the pain. It is snug-
gling close by our side and is eclipsing
all the beauties of life and nature
around us by its dull insistent note.

The magic spell of music may carry us for a little out of ourselves, may temporarily fill our hearts with rest, calm and peace, may silence the voice of a forsaken duty or an unconquered pang of memory, but unless the music inspires us with the wine of new purpose, the vital impelling courage to act as we should, it has been only— musical cocaine. And as we walk the streets homeward, the pain starts afresh as if the very respite had made it want to revenge itself for our forgetting.

If we could pack our worries and anxieties—those restless imps that feed on our happiness and starve our souls— in storage before we set out on a travel tour, change of scene might be of real value to us. It might be a physical upbuilding, a mental refreshing and a moral rebirth. But if our worries are going to camp out in our stateroom at night and keep us awake to listen to what they tell us and to walk the deck with us by day—they prove to us that running away has been a vain flight —not a valorous fight.

If they loom so large before us that they shut out the view of the Alps and darken the skies of sunny Spain—why, we then realize we have not been fighting at all, but merely taking the same old play of our sorrows on a European tour where only the scenery is changed while the cast of emotions is the same.

We constantly tilt at windmills of dis·raction, leaving the real battle on the field of the soul—unfought. Tiring of the friends who have been near to us and whom we disqualify either because they *will* talk about our sorrow or they *will not*, we hunt up acquaintances or semi-friends of the vintage of five years ago and try Society. This is only another brand of cocaine.

We imagine, self-deceptively, that six nights a week in evening dress might of itself banish our sorrow or stifle our secret grief. But what is the use of it all if, when the evening clothes are removed, we find ourselves still in the unremoved strait-jacket of memories we would give aught in the world to escape forever? The intensified pain seems even greater as we contrast our misery with the happiness of others. How do we know that they, too, are not wearing strait-jackets?

We become nervously, morbidly over-sensitive. An innocent chance word may, in an instant, fan into flame the embers of an unconquered pain. Some simple ordinary incident may cause the river of a sleeping emotion to rise suddenly and almost flood the soul. By some subtle electric disturbance in the brain's central office a thousand calls of different new impressions may successively ring violently the bell of the *one* dominating memory that haunts us. Every road of our thought leads inevitably—to the Rome of our grief.

We must just drop our cocaine, stop running away from life, and fight the battle, alone if alone we must—till we rise, sanctified, sweetened and strengthened—a victor on the field of seeming defeat. Each of us has his own special enemies that would take from him the —crown of his individuality.

These are the times when we must stand still for a little, get our bearings through the fumes and the smoke and —face and fight the life that is. Some say change of scene *does* lull, does soothe, does cure. No, Nature may with time help us to forget but it is usually only putting our grief or trial to sleep if—unconquered. We are left too often with scars of morbidness, dead ideals, awful regret. We are not calmed but paralyzed—in certain emotions. We are weakened ; we have lost the possible strength of a victory that would make all future pain easier to bear because of finer character, confidence, and courage.

In assaying our trouble, let us first see if it is really as great as it seems. We often listen to trifles of worry through a microphone of fear, where the footfall of a few flies is exaggerated till it sounds like the battling hoofs of a cavalry charge across a wooden bridge. There are petty cares that we should be ashamed of noticing. Some of them are no larger than a dewdrop that the heat of a few seconds' clear thinking should dissipate into nothingness. These we put under the microscope of our anxiety until a microbe seems as big as a prehistoric monster. Treat these as if they were mere mosquitoes of fate trying to annoy the Sphinx. Learn to look these troubles squarely in the eye, smile bravely, be calm, and say to them —" You never even touched me."

There is one great sorrow in life that carries with it a sacredness that no irreverent hand can touch lightly. It is the sacrifice we have to make on the altar of our love. Love, in some form, is the greatest thing in life—the others are understudies. The saddest hour is the loss of one we hold dear. It is bitterly hard when the loved one still lives but separated forever from us by misunderstanding, injustice, folly—love grown cold. There is that other loss when the one most loved passes from us into the eternal silence.

The death of love transmutes every high light of past joys into agonies of memory by comparison with present deadness. The death of the loved one, with love still strong, crowns their life together and makes past joys sweet, serene and soothing in the Holy of Holies of memory. The first gradually eclipses the memory of joys; the second the memories of sorrows— while intensifying the sweetness of remembered happiness. In either form, it speaks our supreme sorrow, the taking of the last fortress of our courage.

There is one form of distraction that is not—running away from life. It is in seeking to be genuinely interested in the daily lives of others, in growing more unselfish, in heartening others, in standing strong by those in need, in distributing as an administrator to all humanity the estate of love that has been ours—in deeds of cheer, constancy, helpfulness, consolation, kindness and thoughtfulness.

Let us feel, in every sorrow, that there is something within us, a divine spirit that rises superior to all else in life, something imperishable, unperturbed, impregnable—something that can no more be sullied than a ray of sunlight from the heart of the sun.

Let us fight—fight with the certainty of winning a greater, bigger, finer self. We cannot always evade the darker side of life but we can dictate the effect we will permit it to have on us. Let us fight like Jacob of old wrestling with the angel and say, " I will not let thee go unless thou bless me." And the angel of grief always does bless us —if we battle aright. Somehow, somewhere, somewhen, the conquered sorrow is transformed into finer strength, broader sympathy, tested friendships, gentler tolerance, greater charity, and a truer vision of the realities of life.

If our sorrow be inevitable we must bear it bravely so that we may bear it easier. If we can get salvage of hope from the wreck of failure we are lessening the loss. Often a sacrifice of petty pride will bring back all the old happiness. Fight must help; flight—never. Our environment is so largely the radiation of our individuality that we can never truly desert it. Running away from life is merely —a coward's useless alibi.

XVII

The Dark Valley *of* Prosperity

HE great test of individual character is not struggle but attainment; not failure but success; not adversity but prosperity. When Nature wants to put a man through the third degree, she places near him his laurel wreaths of victory; she megaphones to him the world's plaudits of success; she parades stacks of newspaper clippings and magazine articles with his portraits; she clinks his money-bags in his ears, and she tells him confidentially of the world-changing power of his influence. She smiles on him kindly and murmurs, " Poor fellow, is he able to stand it?" Then she sends him for his test through—the dark valley of prosperity.

Few pass through it immune; few acquire no perversion of mind, few escape fractures of ideals or new dents in character. But when *one*, through it all, remains just as good and simple and lovable as when he began the trip, remains kindly, sincere, strong, sympathetic, and unspoiled, Nature is glad indeed to admit she has found —a real man, a big man, a great man.

It is called the dark valley of prosperity because it, so often, dims the vision to the finer realities of life. In the early stages, in the dimness, they cannot see their old friends as they pass. There comes a peculiarity of the extensor muscles which prevents their extending the hand to some one no longer necessary to them. They acquire a form of memory impairment which prevents them remembering past favours and debts of gratitude due to those who stood by them in their hours of need. They do not notice their sudden and increasing chest expansion. They find that their hats are continuously growing too small for them in a singular manner.

In the dark valley, their dearest hopes and their high ideals often slip away—into the silence. For them are substituted avarice and ambition, dressed in a livery of gold, and the individual may near-sightedly mistake them for higher good. In the shadows, conscience, the eye of the soul, becomes, too often, dulled so that it cannot see the distinctions between genuine honour and a dishonour their lawyers inform them is technically legal. They fail, often, in their morally fading vision, to see the difference between right and wrong, between justice and the injustice of misused power. These are but samples of dangers that menace all, but which some overcome.

Sometimes they grope along the way, unconscious of the great price that they are paying. Suddenly they may realize, under a burst of temporary sunlight in the valley, that they have somehow, somewhere lost love, sympathy, trust, confidence, sweetness of nature or something else that has been —dearest in the world to them. It has dropped away in the darkness like a locket from an unguarded chain, and they may—never find it again.

It is sheer cant that would throw

wealth, fame, prosperity and success into a moral dust-heap as vanities of the world.   We all want them.   Those who take a high moral pose against them are either envious or are elbowing their way to get front Pharisee seats in the temple of virtue.   These things are not evil in themselves. They are great powers for good but they are not—life's greatest.   They are less than the real joys, like love, that —no money can buy.   Their wrong is when acquired by a sacrifice of truth, honour, justice or the real virtues of life, or when they are misused or consecrated to the selfish side of living. Their danger is in the corrupting effect the individual can hardly ever keep them from having on him.

Poverty, struggle, failure and adversity are not in themselves passports to saintship—though they have given moral strength and sweetness to thousands. They have their own hard, bitter temptations to meet face to face. Theirs is far from an easy fight—the daily hand-to-hand battle with fate. But their temptations are usually direct, bold, clearly defined and their joys require so little. The tempting tests of prosperity come in subtle phases, gilded, perfumed, masking in deceptive guise.

Poverty knows the word "stealing"; wealth may think it "financeering." Poverty knows "envy of another's possessions"; wealth may assume taking a manufacturing plant as "a good business deal." It may then even, by some strange sophistry, justify itself by declaring they will do better for the people. Poverty knows hunger for bread; wealth may hunger for the money of the bread-earners. Poverty usually sees evil in its aggressive, hardest phases. Prosperity may find it hidden and unsuspected like Cleopatra's asp in a bouquet of flowers. "For one who can stand prosperity," says Carlyle, "one hundred can stand adversity."

A very slight drop of the acid of prosperity will begin the revelation of character of the man—be he not big enough to be simple. The slightest elevation in position, the least new good fortune, some temporary elation may reveal it. Have you ever noticed the man who has made a bit of a success in the city and returns for a week to his native village? He says he has come back to see the folks but it is really to have the folks see hir

He enjoys the envy he excites in those who have not, like him—lived in the city. He wants to get sunburned in the warmth and fervour of their admiration. He stretches at length in his tilted chair, locks his thumbs behind the armholes of his waistcoat, and plays a flute solo of vanity on his breast-bone, using the buttons as stops manipulated by his fingers.

He occupies the centre of the stage every minute with his monologue. There is a touch of swagger in his walk, an irritating undertone of tolerance and patronage in his speech, and that loud voice we involuntarily use with the deaf. He is his own Boswell and his own Gabriel. It is, perhaps, only a harmless brand of vanity, but it shows he is getting near to the entrance of—the dark valley. When a

big, simple man of *real* fame comes
back, the story of what *he* has done
—usually leaks out incidentally ; it is
not exploded like a bomb.

The author of a successful book may
have won his honours because he wrote
with serious purpose.   His message was
supreme—fee for delivery, secondary.
But he may be attacked by the vertigo
of money-making and forget every-
thing else.   Inspired by his publisher,
he may galvanize an old earlier book
of his youth or rush through a hasty
new one to have it in print before the
wave of his sudden fame has died on
the shores of forgetfulness.   He talks
less now of art and more of mart.   The
new book may fail because he fell into
the pitfall of commercialism in—the
dark valley of prosperity.

Successful artists and illustrators, in

many instances, do not follow up the
first successes that won them fame.
They slur over their work ; they stand
still or they degenerate. They accentu-
ate the superficial in their style and
care little for the strength that once
was vital. They repeat the same char-
acters, merely in slightly changed posi-
tions, like a cheap stock-company with
a small cast and a meagre wardrobe,
—playing in repertoire. These men
often say if one ventures to speak that
kindly word of protest we should
always give to the needy : " Oh, what
difference does it make—it pays all
right." They should find some good
Samaritan to drag them from the dark
valley of prosperity and put them back
again in the sunlight of struggle and
the inspiration of adversity.

The business man who began in a

small way and suddenly finds fortune emptying cornucopias of gold into his lap may find it hard to keep his feet and not to lose his head. The demon of greed may transform him—he wants more. He is like the farmer who desired only the land that adjoined his farm—each addition increased the field of desire ; the more he had the more he wanted. Then may come a million owning a man, not the man a million. To accumulate more, he may defy laws, bribe legislatures and buy judges. Like a modern Joshua, he seeks to command —the sun of justice to stand still. He chloroforms his business conscience until it sleeps so soundly that an earthquake would not jostle it.

Wealth often makes men who started in bravely with high ideals, and normal moral health, become cold, heartless, selfish and uncharitable as they walk through the dark valley of prosperity. They often become arrogant and have a tendency to expect argument to close when they speak. They seem to have a corner on judgment as if their eye alone saw the sun of truth, their wisdom alone plumbed the depth of great questions. The abnormal pressure of business often forces them into pleasures of which they count not the cost nor the character. They are often too busy to take stock of the goods of their soul. The culture of the higher affections and sentiments is often killed. The very intensity of their work or their play produces a yawning, yearning ennui hard to overcome.

Trifles affect them strangely they grow irritated, impatient, irrational, at finding even a crumpled rose-leaf in

the golden couch of their insomnia.
They become more and more suspicious,
and hardly know whom to trust.
They fear every one is paving the way
for some deal ; stealthily seeking to gain
their influence or to subtract something
from the useless pile of their surplus
wealth.   They can have but few
trusted, genuine friends of the mind,
heart and soul.   Great wealth, like
genius, isolates man from his fellows in
the—closest harmonies of life.

Let us live so gladly and glowingly
in the sunlight of real simple love that
means our great all ; with faith in those
few around us that girdles our whole
world, realizing the sweetness of honest
true friendships that so inspire ; happy
in the noble round of loyalty, consecra-
ting to-day's duties to usher in a finer
to-morrow, so living in the joy of our

simple life on the purer lines of un-
selfish realness that—we shall be glad
the trials, tests and temptations of the
dark valley have actually snubbed us
as too unimportant to notice.

If called upon to the burdens of the
greater responsibility let us bear them
bravely at our best and let nothing rob
us of simplicity, sweetness, strength,
sympathy and all that is sterling. The
greatest men and women are ever the
simplest. There are thousands who
bear their great burdens of fame, suc-
cess, power, prosperity or wealth and
who remain happy as of old and little,
if any, spoiled by it all. They must
truly be rare characters, of fine re-
sources of thought, heart, nature and
soul who can retain the crown of their
individuality after a journey through
—the dark valley of prosperity.

4

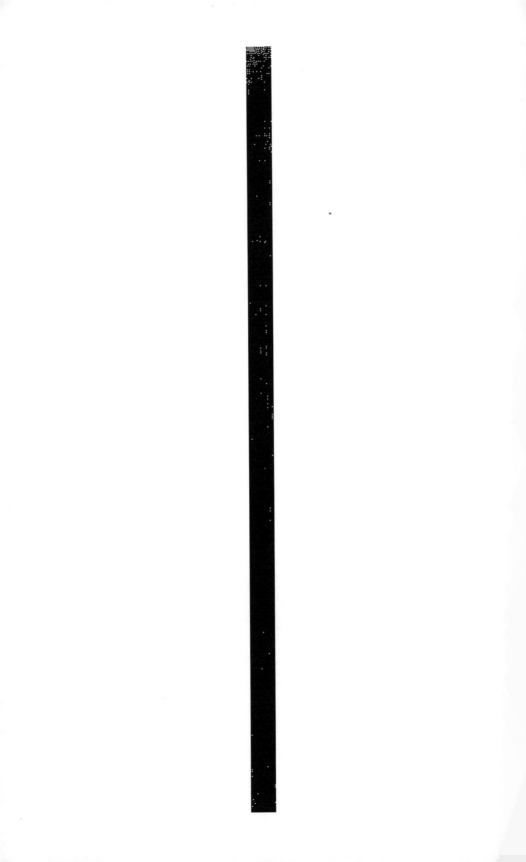

20281422R00122

Made in the USA
Lexington, KY
01 February 2013